Islam & Science for Starters

Learn Science with the Quran

Astronomy

Geology

Biology

Shariq Ali Khan

YouTube videos, click/type

https://www.youtube.com/channel/UCnGjHQovUXZ-llgiegZcUTQ

Or point phone camera to

Content:

Part 1 Universe, Pages 3-18

Universe, Big Bang, Smoke, Expansion, Planets, Stars, Supernovae, Elements

Part 2 Solar System, Pages 19-40

Sun, Moon, Stars, Planets, Eclipses, Solar System, Night, and Day

Part 3 Earth, Pages 41-61

Atmosphere, Interior, Layers, Faults, Mountains, Depth, Drift, Earthquakes

Part 4 Water, Pages 62-82

Water-cycle, Rivers, Oceans, Basins, Vents, Depth, Waves, Elements

Part 5 Animals, Pages 83-106

Evolution = Creation, Timescale, Forms and Shapes, Genetics, Development

Part 6 Humans, Pages 107-129

Origin, Creation, Evolution, The Ark, Embryology, Development

Part 7/ 5 Pillars, Pages 130-171

Faith, Prayer, Charity, Fasting, Pilgrimage, Invitation, Peace, Justice

Part 1
Astronomy
Universe

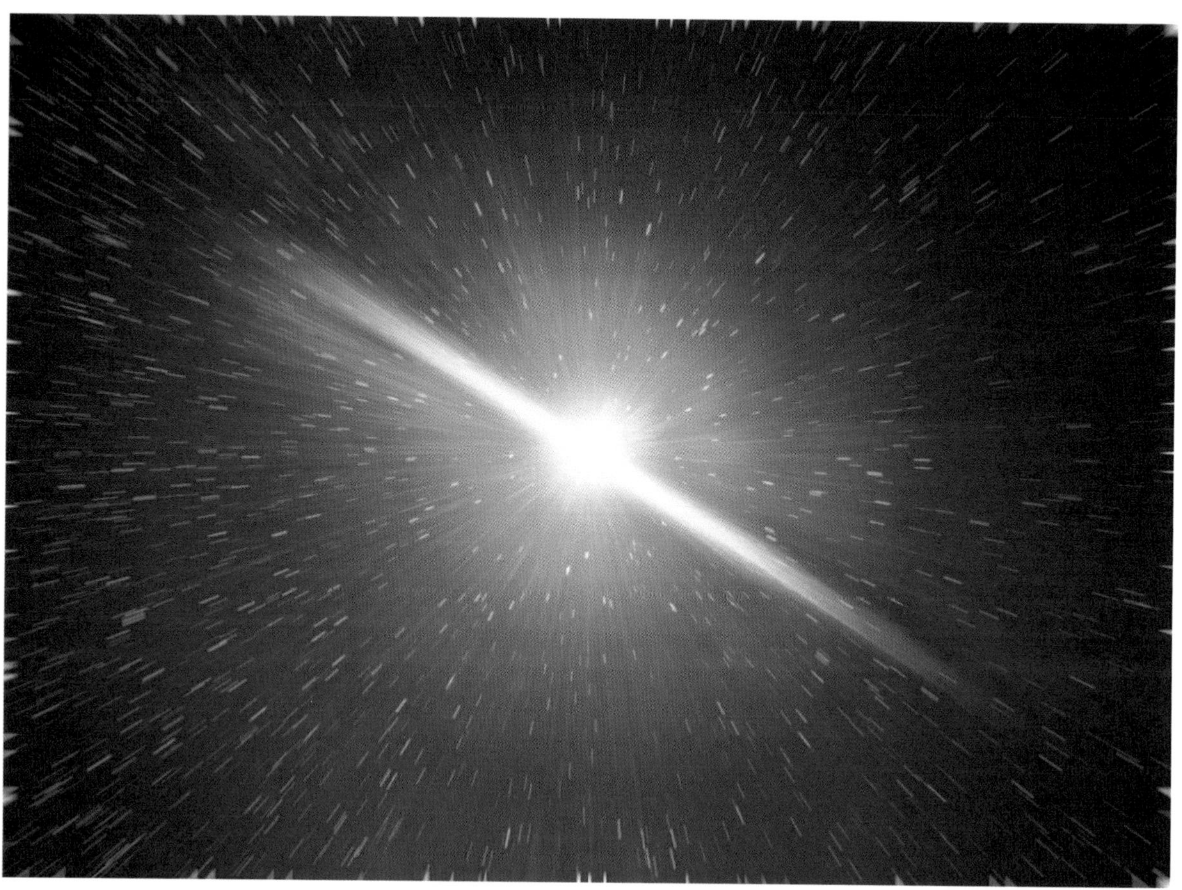

In the name of Allah, the Most Forgiving, Most Merciful.

In the Quran Allah asks:

"Do not the Unbelievers see that the Heavens and the Earth were joined together before I tore them apart...?"

Surah Al-Anbiyaa, 21 Ayah 30

The Quran is 1400 years old, and scientists have just found out now that it was exactly like that. They call this event the...

..Big Bang...

Shortly after the Big Bang, the universe was like smoke.

Through the Big Bang Allah made time, space, matter, movement, and gravity also came into existence. Before there was no such thing. This means that outside the universe there is eternity. We can now understand that Allah is eternal because He created time. He is everlasting. So, He was not created, and He has created everything.

Allah commanded
"... the sky and it had been smoke: He said to it and the Earth: 'Come together willingly or unwillingly!' They said: 'We come together in obedience."
Surah Ha Mim As Sajdah, 41 Ayah 11

So, the sun, the moon, the planets, and also our Earth are all Believers because they listen to the Almighty and obey him. We should do the same.

The smoke is made of H (Hydrogen) and He (Helium).

Scientists know now that the universe used to be like smoke because far away galaxies are like smoke and incredibly old.

The planets and other bodies in the universe are made out of this smoke. The rest is empty space, which is also called a vacuum. Air is not a vacuum because it has gasses that we can breathe. Such gas is O2, oxygen. We cannot breathe in outer space.

The first atoms were H, hydrogen, and He, helium. They are also the most widespread elements in the universe.

Sky, Earth, Sun, Moon, and Stars are Believers...

The Sky and the Earth follow the command of Allah. They are Believers. So is everyone and everything when they are born. But some people don't want to be Believers and don't follow Allah's command. The Big Bang happened a long time ago. Today the universe has planets, like our Earth, moons like our moon, stars like our sun, solar systems, like our own, and galaxies, like our own galaxy which our solar system is part of.

There is much more to be found in the universe...

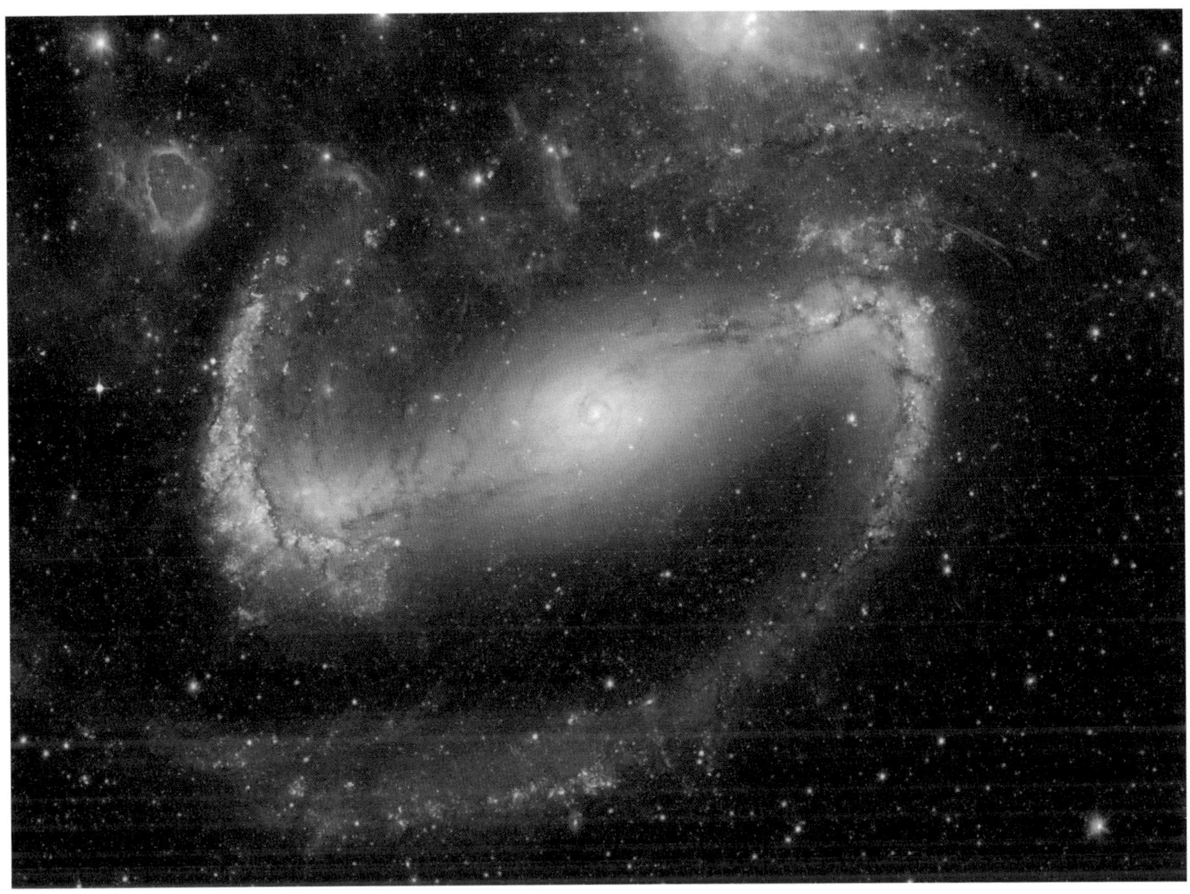

If we look through telescopes, we can see distant stars and galaxies which are just as old as the universe. They are also enormously large.

This smoke-formation looks like the head of a horse and is called the horse-head nebula. There are all types of shapes in the universe!

This is the Hubble-Telescope...

...you can look back 14 billion years into the past with it!

Now there’s a new telescope called Webb. What will it show us?

14 billion years refers to light-years which is a measurement of distance. The distance that light covers in 1 year is 1 light-year. It is not a measurement of time!

Red light in faraway galaxies shows us that the universe is still growing.

It is worth mentioning that the speed of light is encoded in the Quran. You should search for it yourself. Also, the numerology of the Quran is very detailed and enlightening. It is based on the number 19 and a symmetry of the alphabets and verses. There are free books and information about it on the Internet, just like about the Speed of Light in the Quran.

Allah also says in the Quran:

"I have built the heaven with might, and it is I who makes it grow forever."

Surah Az-Zariyat, 51 Ayah 47

Red light has less energy than other light and proves to scientists that distant galaxies are still moving away, and the universe is expanding endlessly. We can see this through the Hubble-Telescope which has been in the orbit for over 30 years.

The Big Bang and the Expansion are new discoveries.

Scientists agree that all stars and planets were joined together in an extremely small and dense space and then exploded as shown in the picture with the Big Bang.

Scientists have only discovered the growth of the universe and the Big Bang now. Allah said this in the Quran 1400 years ago already.

This makes our belief in Allah stronger.

So, we should read the Quran because there is no God other than Allah.

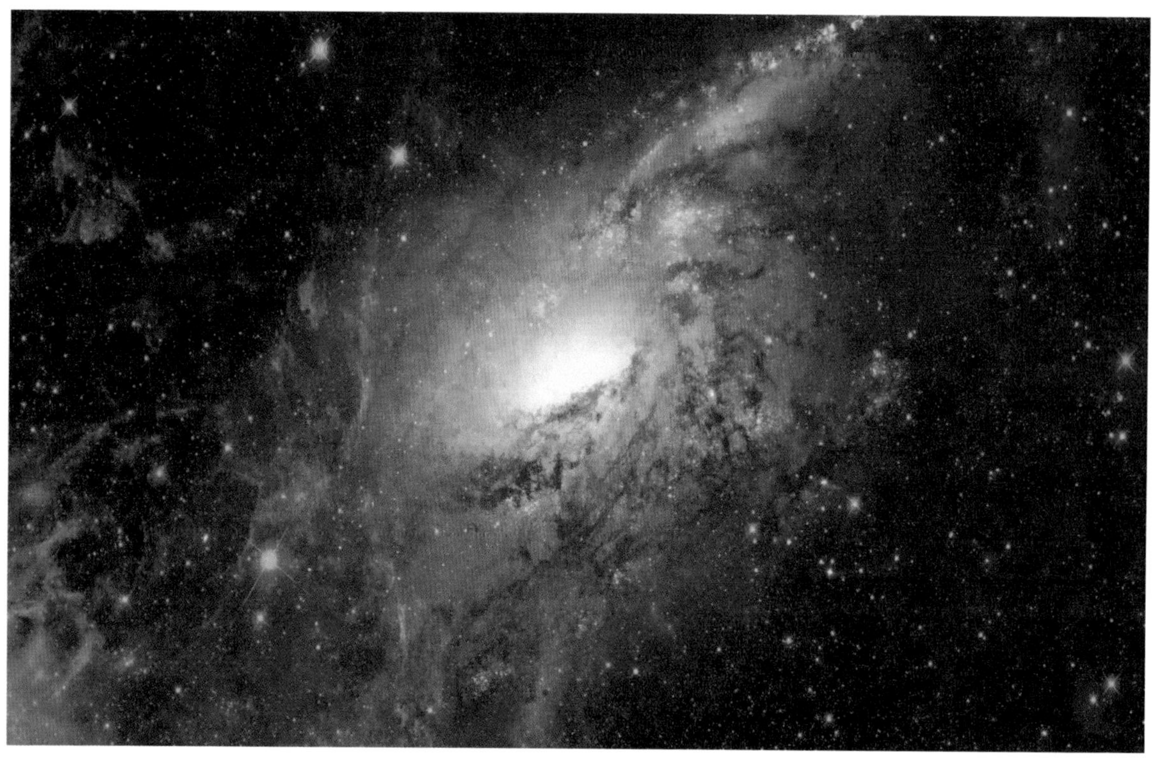

Supernovae are large distant stars, and they are extremely hot!

The Supernovae are important for life.

Inside the Supernovae H (Hydrogen) and He (Helium) is turned into Fe, which is the chemical sign for iron. This process is called nuclear fusion. After this, the Supernovae send out bodies called meteorites. These meteorites fall on planets like our Earth and make it rich in iron and other elements which are important for life.

This is how our Earth which was once smoke and then liquid has become hard as it is now...

This is how a Supernova looks when it becomes old. It explodes and sends out meteorites.

That's why Allah says:

"...I sent down Iron with which you can make (material for) mighty war as well as many good things for mankind..."

Surah Al-Hadid, 57 Ayah 25

...and He says...

"Soon I will show them my Signs in the (furthest) regions and their souls until it becomes clear to them that this is the truth..."

Surah Ha-Mim, 41 Ayah 53

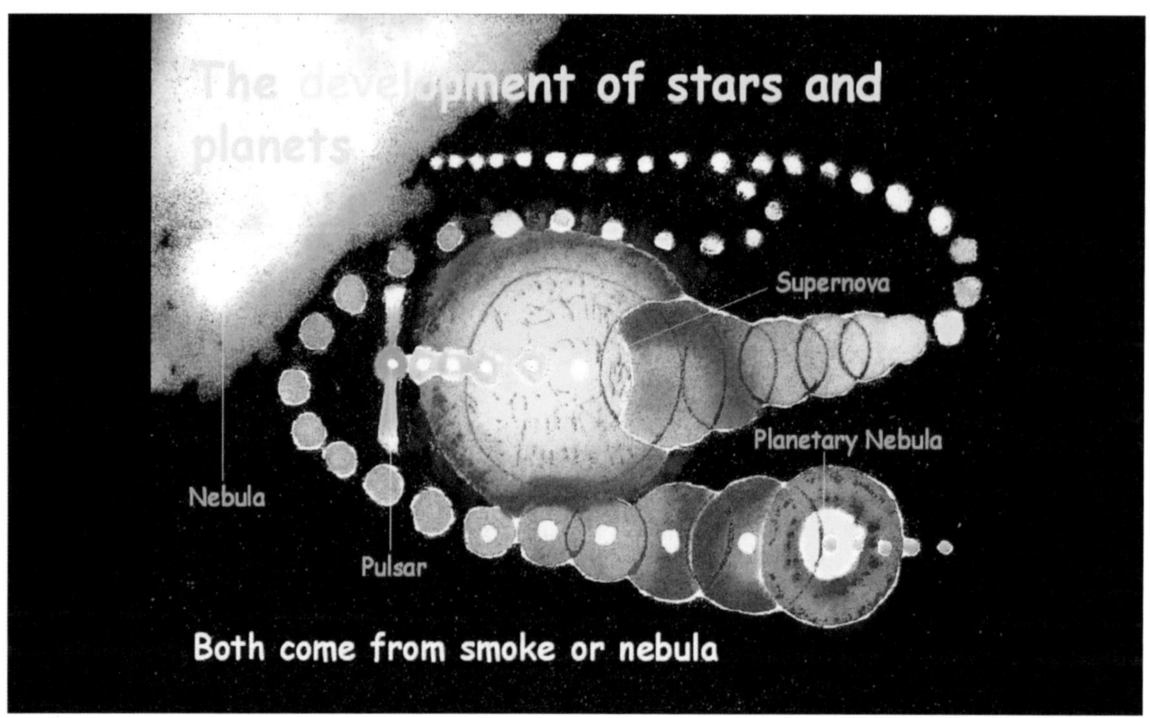

The development of stars and planets:

Nebula

Pulsar

Supernova to Star

Planetary Nebula

Both, planets, and stars, like our sun, come from smoke or nebula.

A typical nebula, smoke formation in the distant universe.

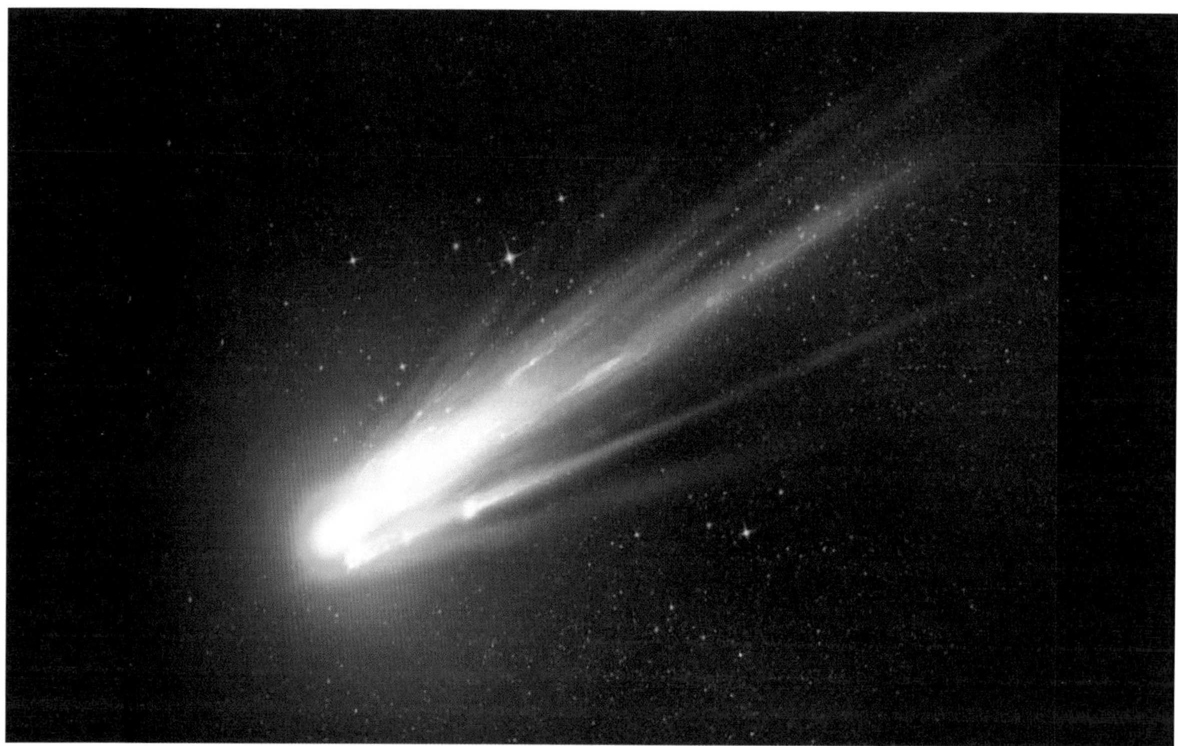

Comets move through the universe. They carry iron, copper and other heavy elements and minerals which were created inside the Supernovae.

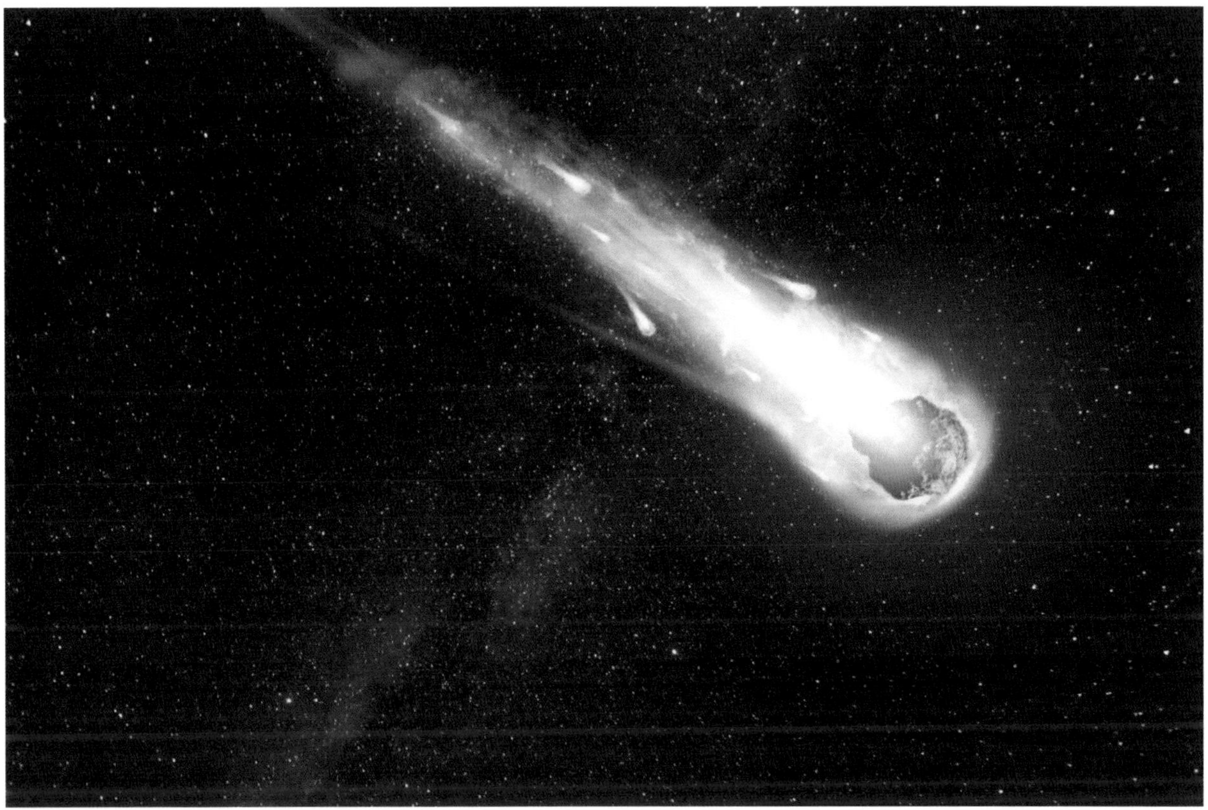

Their colour can tell you what they are made of. Red is iron, blue is copper, yellow is gas.

"...I sent down Iron with which you can make (material for) mighty war as well as many good things for mankind..."

Surah Al-Hadid, 57 Ayah 25

It is curious that if we look at the periodic table of elements, the Surah and Ayah number above closely match that of iron (Fe). In fact, the overall number of stable elements is also very near to 114, the overall number of Surahs in the Quran! This cannot be mere coincidence and more reseearch needs to be done into the numbers of Ayaht and Surahs and the different elements and their isotopes. The elements above 114 are very unstable and exisit only for fractions of a second

Summary:

In the Quran, Allah has told us exactly how the universe is built. It is his creation.

There are details about the Big Bang. Shortly after the Big Bang, there was smoke, which was built up of Hydrogen and Helium. The bodies in the universe came together out of the same material as this smoke. Therefore, the planets are also made from this smoke. We live on such a planet. It is called the Earth. In the Quran Allah also explains that he makes the universe grow. Allah also describes to us in the Quran that he sent down elements like iron. This happened inside giant stars which are extremely far away. Scientists call these Supernovae which explode when they are incredibly old. Then comets and meteors burst out of it. Scientists have discovered all these things in the 20th century and the Hubble-Telescope has helped scientists in proving much of this. The Hubble-Telescope is only around 30 years old. The Quran was revealed to the Prophet Mohammed (peace be on him) 1400 years ago at a time when telescopes, spaceships, and satellites did not exist. It covers many aspects of natural phenomena in modern science. The Quran is a revelation of Allah, who is the Creator of all things and beings. These are just a few of His signs. There are many more.

There is no God other than Allah,
and Mohammed is the Messenger of Allah.

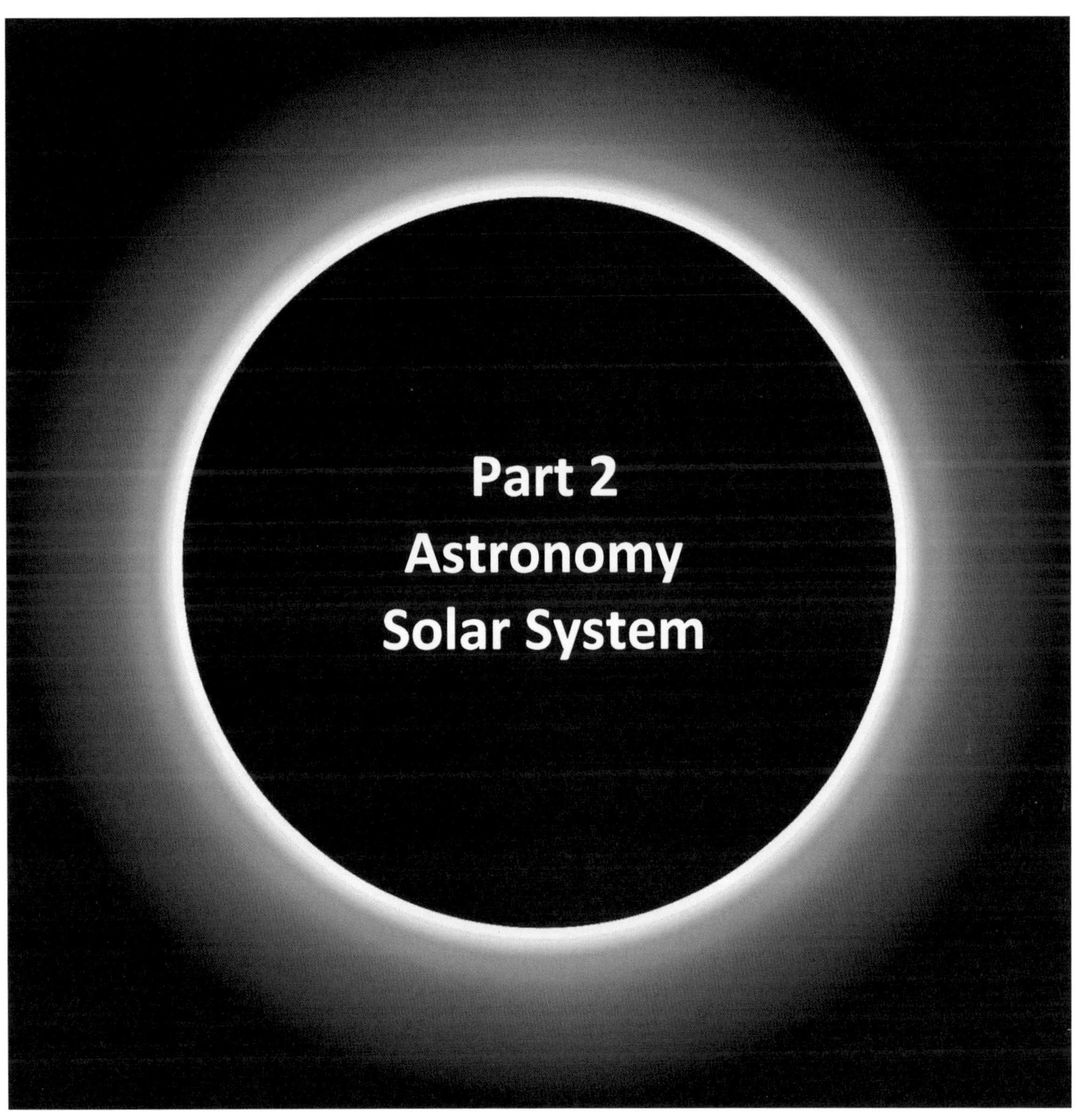
Part 2
Astronomy
Solar System

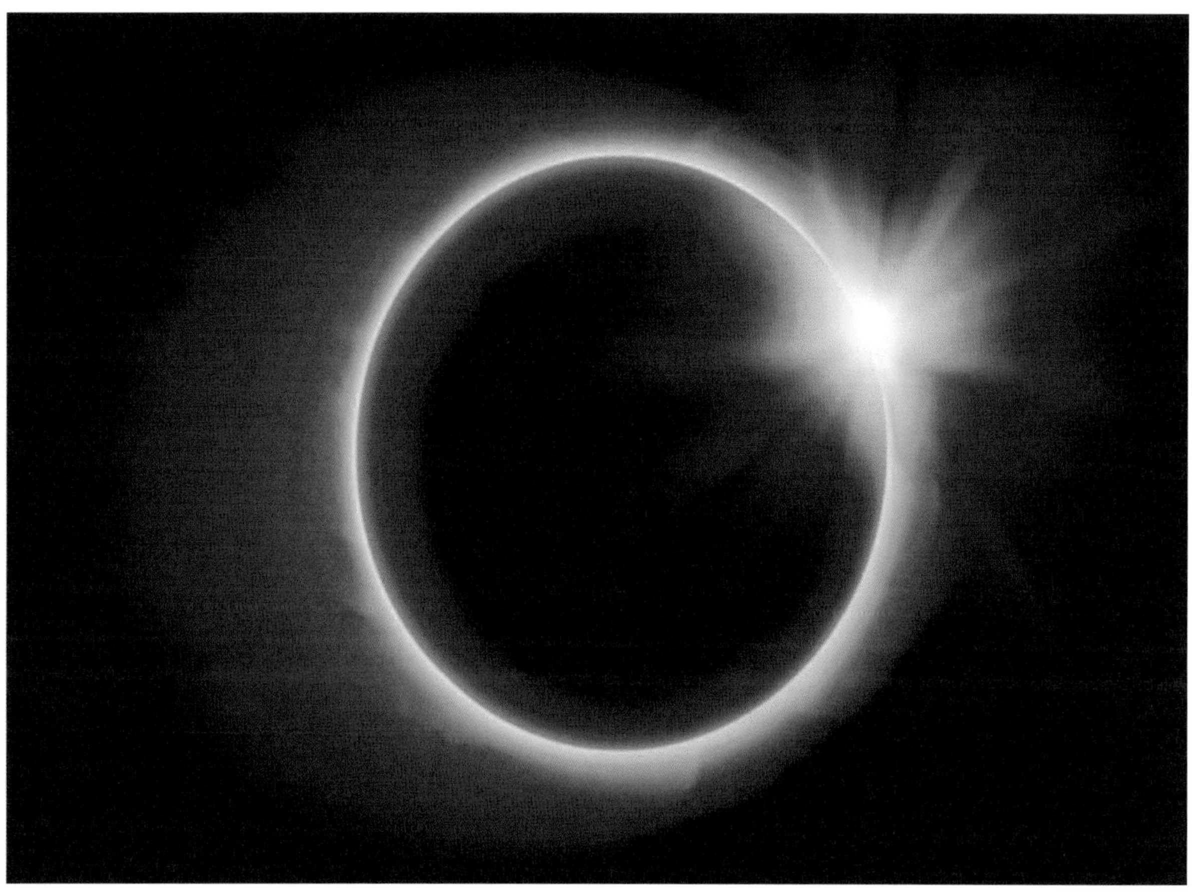

In the name of Allah, The Most Forgiving, Most Merciful.

In the Quran Allah says:

"I made the moon a light in their midst and the sun a Lamp"
(Surah Noah 71, Ayah 16)

The Quran is 1400 years old, and scientists found out much later that the moon has no light of its own and reflects the light of the sun.

So, the sun is a source of light, the moon isn't. This difference was not known at the time when the Quran came. Allah sent the Quran and made everything.

The sun and the moon are very different

The sun has a lot of energy. It is very big. Its weight keeps it from falling apart. There is a lot of Hydrogen and Helium on the sun, and everything is broken down into very small pieces, smaller than atoms (so called plasma).

The sun is sending out energy in form of light and heat to us and across the solar system. It is a lamp, which means, it is a source of light.

The moon is made of cold and solid rock and has very little energy. It reflects the sun's light.

"And I made the moon a light in their midst and the sun a lamp"

(Surah Noah, 71 Ayah 16)

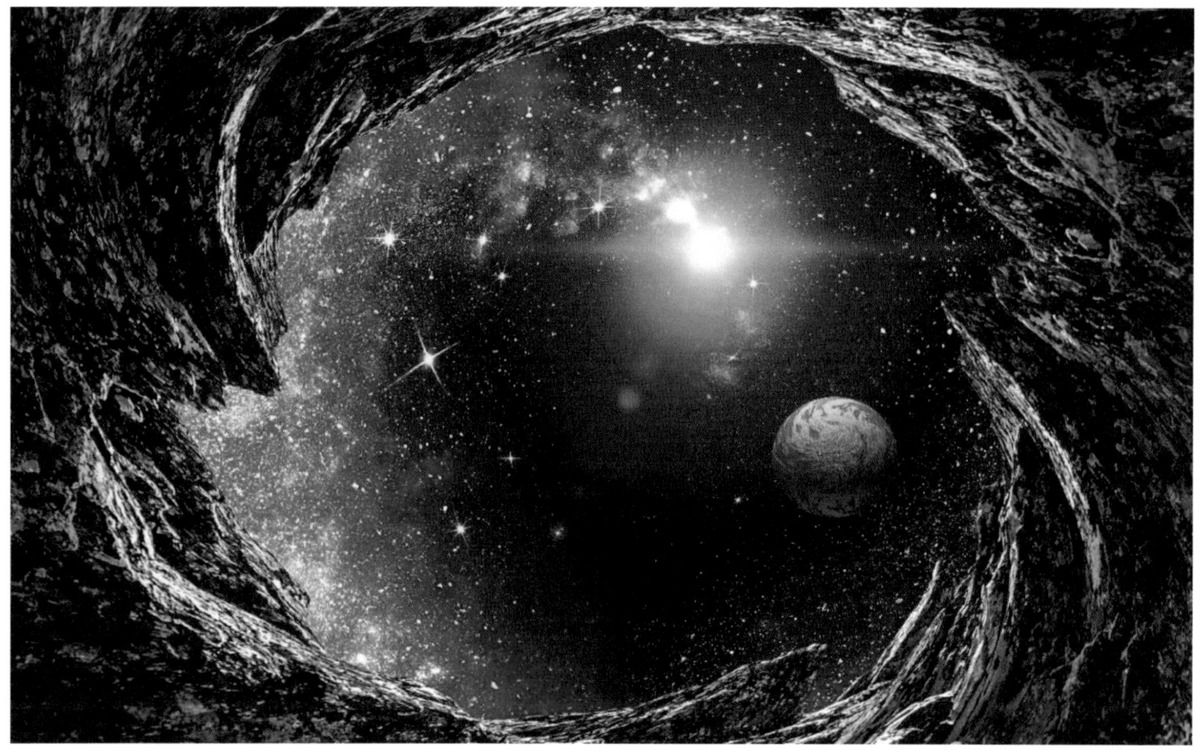

Allah also says about himself:

"...He has ordered the sun and the moon! Each runs for an end. "

Surah Ar-Ra'd 13, Ayah 2

This is another fact that was not known at the time of the Prophet Mohammed (peace be upon him) when the Quran was revealed to him.

The Quran is Allah's last message to us. We should read it, understand it and do what Allah tells us. The sun and the moon are doing it already.

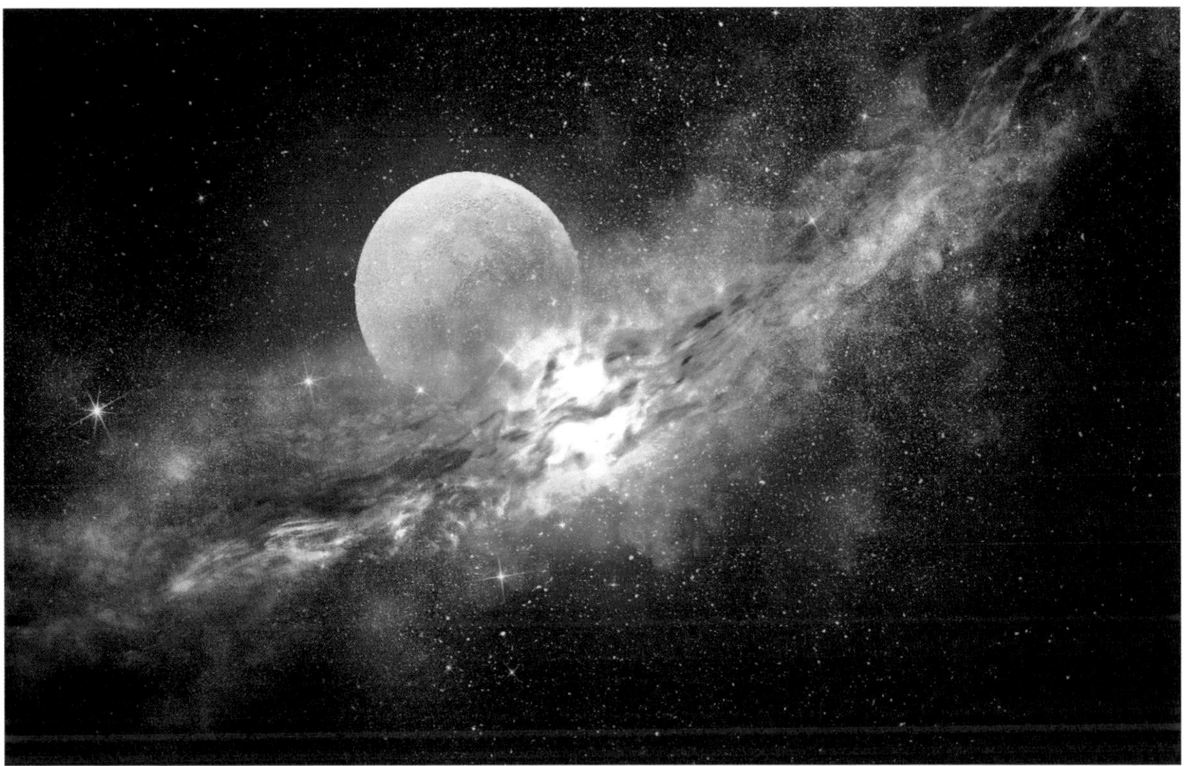

Both sun and moon are moving

Scientists have only found out about 100 years ago that the sun and the moon both together with the whole of our solar-system will crash into a very distant Galaxy called the Dog-system.

The Quran is the true word of the Creator to mankind.

We also must study science and invent useful things as Allah commands us in the Quran.

In Surah Ha-Mim, 41 Ayah 10, Allah orders heaven and Earth to come together from smoke

10 Billion years ago: 5 Billion years ago:

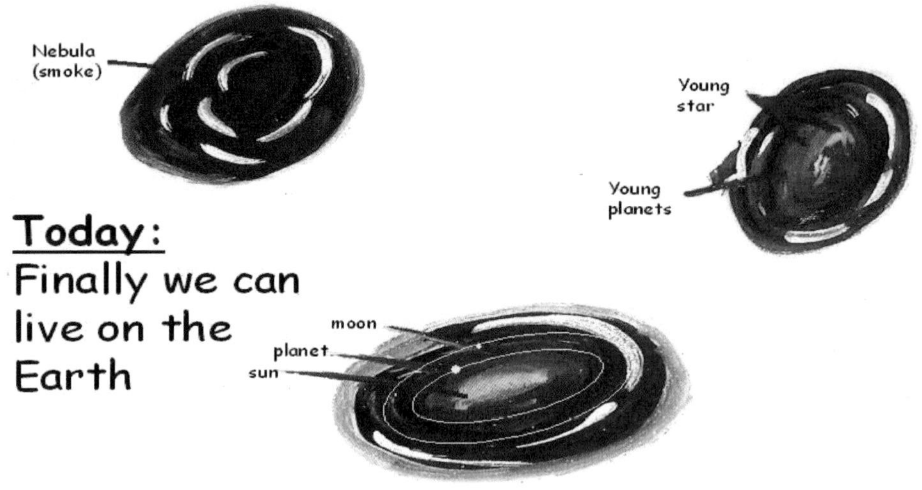

In Surah Ha-Mim 41, Ayah 10, Allah orders heaven and Earth to come together from smoke

10 Billion years ago:

Nebula (smoke)

5 Billion years ago:

Young star

Young planets

Today:

Finally, we can live on the Earth.

Moon, planet, sun

Today, the moon has different stages. This is because the shadow of the Earth covers it from different angles.

It goes from full, over half to less than a quarter of its size and then even smaller. Finally, appears totally. Afterward, it returns again as a tiny sickle. One period like this is called a lunar month.

These stages influence life on Earth and the tide of the oceans: Allah has made sun and moon, so we can measure time through their movement.

(Surah Yunus 10, Ayah 5)

We couldn't measure time without the sun and the moon.

The sun is exactly 400 times larger in diameter and also 400 times farther away than the moon. In this way, the sun looks just as big from the Earth as the moon.

Therefore, solar eclipses are possible on Earth when the moon comes in between Earth and the sun. It is a delicate balance. In a lunar eclipse, the shadow of the Earth nearly covers the moon when the Earth moves in between the moon and sun. Eclipses are signs of Allah, the Almighty.

Eclipses are only possible on Earth and connected with the appearance of intelligent life. Prophet Mohammed (peace be upon him) prayed during eclipses. We should do the same.

Here is the view of a lunar eclipse

Allah also described in the Quran 1400 years ago that the sun is moving around the centre of the galaxy just like the moon around the Earth. Until 200 years ago people thought that the sun stands still.

"...the sun and the moon: all swim along, each in its rounded course."

Surah Al-Anbiyaa 21, Ayah 33

"It is not permitted to the Sun to catch up the Moon nor can the Night outstrip the Day: each moves along in its orbit."
Surah Ya-Sin, 36 Ayah 40
Geocentric
Heliocentric

This are two different models of the solar system from the past. Both turned out to be wrong.

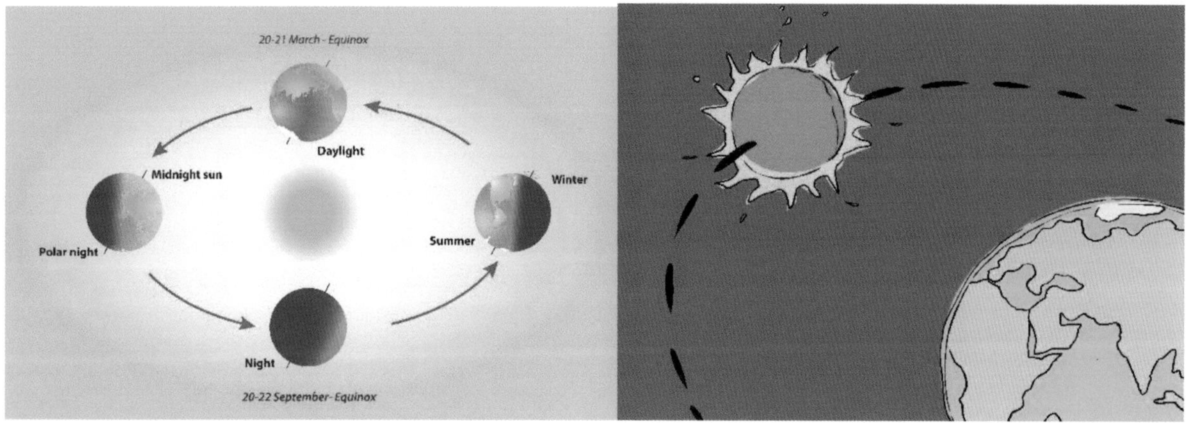

Allah ordered the sun and moon

The picture shows us two different models of the solar system, which were popular 300 years ago.

One is from the Catholic Church, the geocentric view, which says that everything turns around the Earth (left). The other one says that the sun is motionless in the centre, and everything turns around it. That is the heliocentric view which is also wrong.

The Earth moves around the sun, but the sun also moves around the centre of the galaxy.

All bodies move, just like Allah said in the Quran 1400 years ago. Allah knows all, even the unknown.

"He coils night over day and coils day over night"
Surah Az-Zumar 39, Ayah 5

Allah tells us that the Earth is a ball (sphere) since he coils the night over the day and the day over the night just like a turban is coiled around a head.

The Earth is a ball (sphere) just like a head and the sun's light can only hit it from one side.

The Almighty tells us:

"It is I who made the sun a shining glory and the moon a light and measured out stages for it so that you might know the number of years and how to count time."
Surah Yunus 10, Ayah 5

We know today that without Allah giving us the movement and stages of the sun (day and year and the moon (night and lunar month) we would never have been able to measure time.

Sun and moon serve Allah. We should do that too.

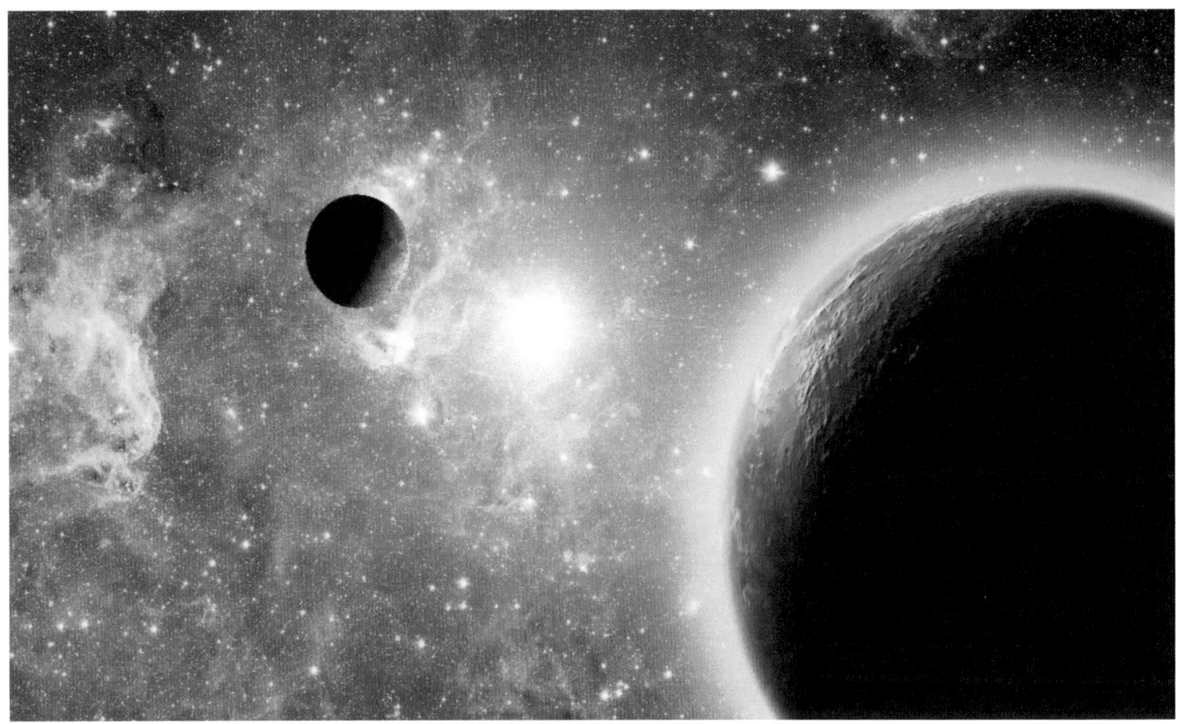

Only now we have found out that...

...the moon reflects the light of the sun and brightens up certain nights in different stages in the shadow of the Earth. The Quran distinguishes the light of the sun and the moon. The Bible doesn't! Many things depend on this like the fertility of animals and plants, the breeding seasons, eclipses and the tide of the oceans. But the moon is not the light source, not the lamp, but a small light. It is a reflection of the sun as it is described in the Quran 1400 years ago.

Much more is to be discovered and we must get involved so we can help mankind and nature.

Allah mentions two types of planet-like bodies in the Quran:

"So verily I call to witness the bodies (Khunnas) that rise and set"

Surah At-Takwir, Surah 81 Ayah 15/16

"When Joseph said unto his father: O my father! Lo! I saw in a dream eleven planets (Kawakib) and the sun and the moon, I saw them prostrating themselves to me."

Surah Yusuf, Surah 12 Ayah 4

Every star, like our sun, has planets which turn around it. This is called a solar system.

What does Allah mean by that?

The planets that rise and set are the comets which travel across many different solar systems and return regularly like Haley's comet in 1986. We can see them for a while and then they are gone for long.

The eleven planets mentioned in the other verse of the Quran are the nine planets of our solar system and two planets that have recently been discovered.

The furthest two common planets have a strange movement. This tells us that there must be more planets disturbing them. They are even thought to be bigger than the commonly known Pluto.

A picture of our solar system with planets a comet and the sun.

11 planets, 2 just discovered after 2000!

Our star, the Sun

Planets:

Mercury

Venus

Earth

Mars

Asteroids (formerly Ceres)

Jupiter

Saturn

Uranus

Neptune

Pluto

Lately discovered Eris

There are many different types of universal bodies in the Quran:

Khunnas, kawakib, tariq, shams, qamar and najm, are the words for heavenly bodies in the Quran.

The Khunnas appear and disappear. They are the comets. The kawakib are planets, like our Earth. Najm is a star. Tarig is a very bright night-or morning-star, in fact a planet, like Venus. Shams is the sun and Qamar is the moon.

These bodies are clearly distinguished by their appearance and roles in the Quran. The Quran is 1400 years old but the discoveries are new. The Quran contains the truth.

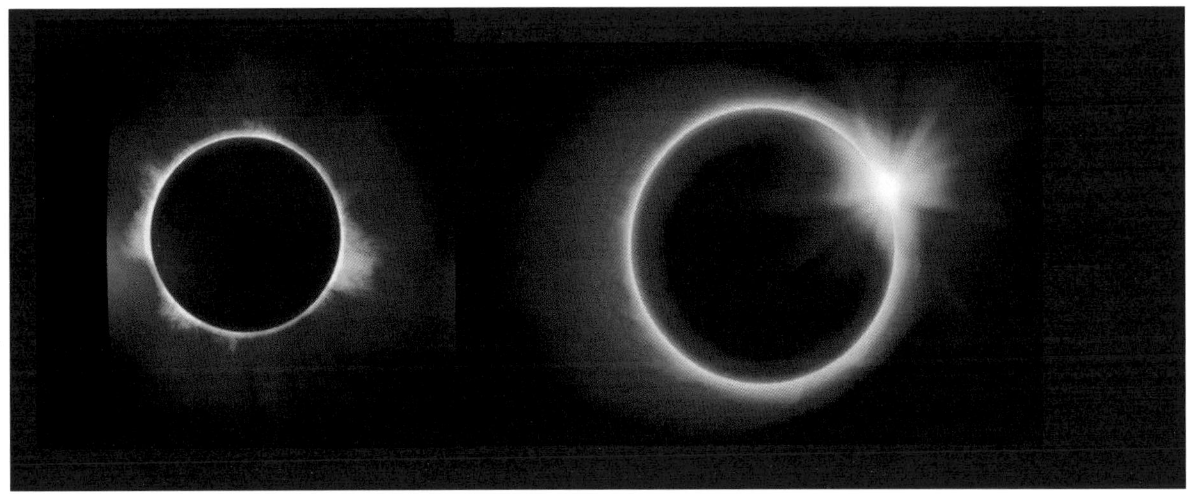

Summary 1

In the Quran, Allah has revealed details about the sun, the moon, the planets, the comets, and the stars, which are all his creations.

There are details about the light of the sun, the light of the moon, and the difference between sun and moon," their movement, the count of time, the stages of the moon, the shape of the Earth and the making of day and night. All these are Allah signs for men so they can believe in him.

There are also verses about the comets, the structure and movement of the solar system, and the number of planets.

Summary: 2

These are scientific discoveries of the last centuries. Scientists have discovered these phenomena using strong telescopes invented less than 300 years ago.

The Quran was revealed to the Prophet Mohammed (peace be on him) 1400 years ago at a time when telescopes, spaceships and satellites did not exist. It covers many aspects of natural phenomena in modern science.

The Quran is a revelation from Allah, the Creator.

These are only a few of His signs. There are many more...

There is no God other than Allah,

and Mohammed is the Messenger of Allah.

Part 3
Geology
Earth

In the name of Allah, the Most Forgiving, Most Merciful.

In the Quran Allah says about himself:

"His design included the heavens for He gave order and perfection to the 7 firmaments"
Surah Al-Baqara 2, Ayah 29

The Quran is 1400 years old and scientists have just now found out that it is exactly like that. There are seven layers of the atmosphere that are clearly different in their nature.

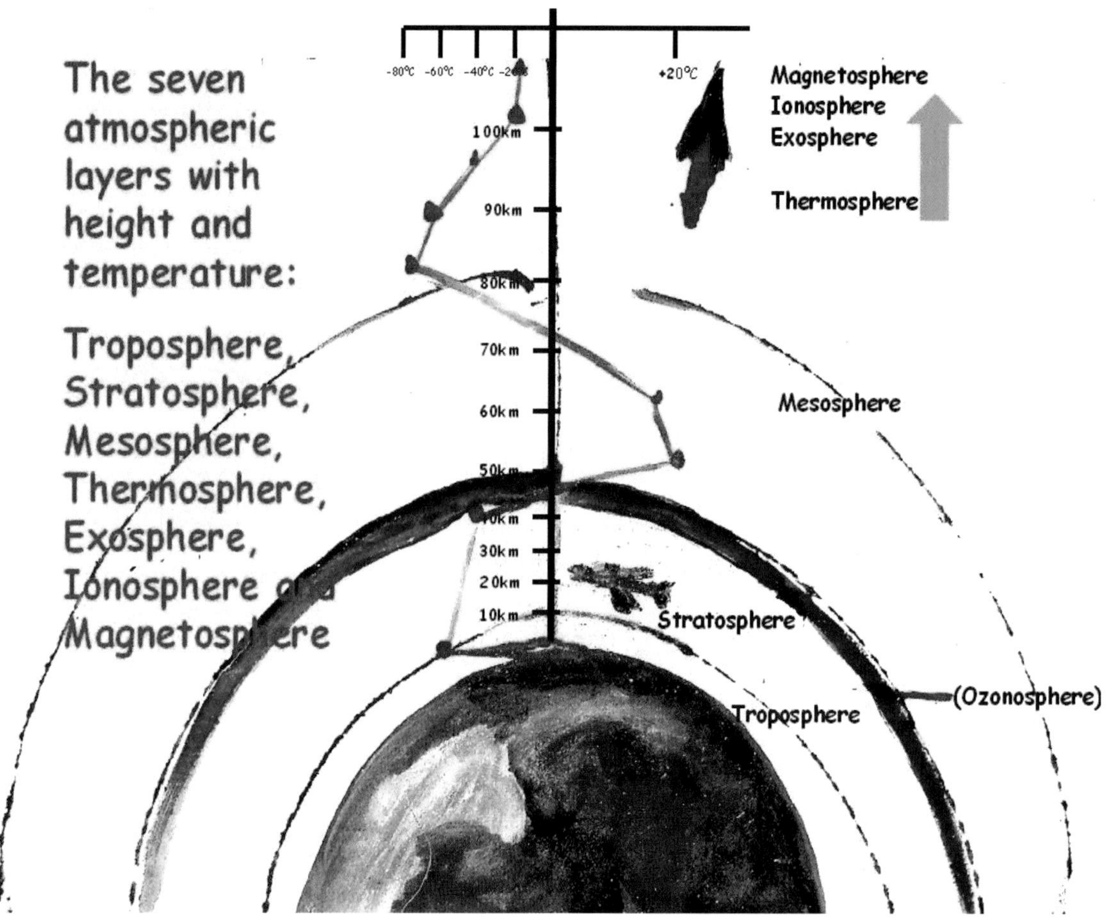

The seven atmospheric layers with height and temperature:

Troposphere,

Stratosphere (Ozonosphere),

Mesosphere,

Thermosphere,

Exosphere,

Ionosphere,

Magnetosphere

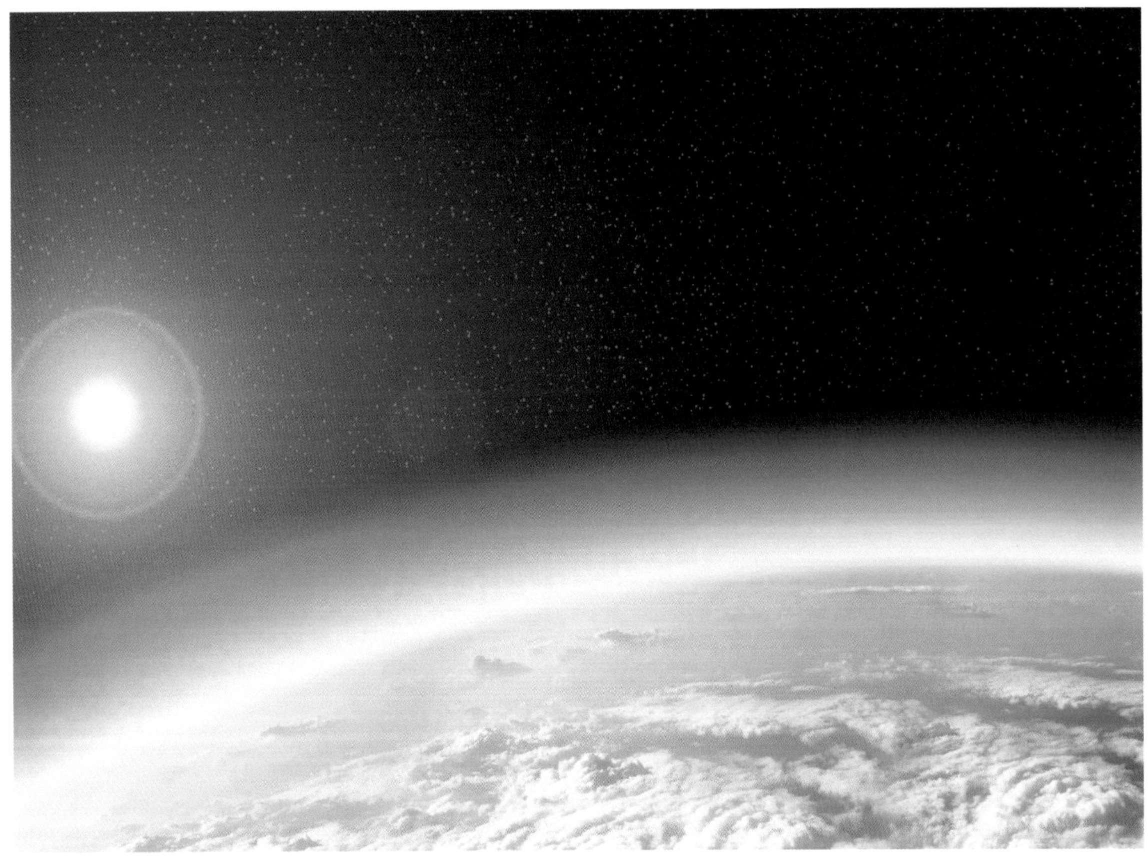

Allah created

"He completed them as 7 heavens (layers) in 2 Days and He assigned to each layer its duty and command."
Surah Ha-Mim 41, Ayah 12

Scientists now know that the atmosphere came into being towards the end of the Earth's evolution and that each of the seven layers has an important function for the protection of life on Earth.

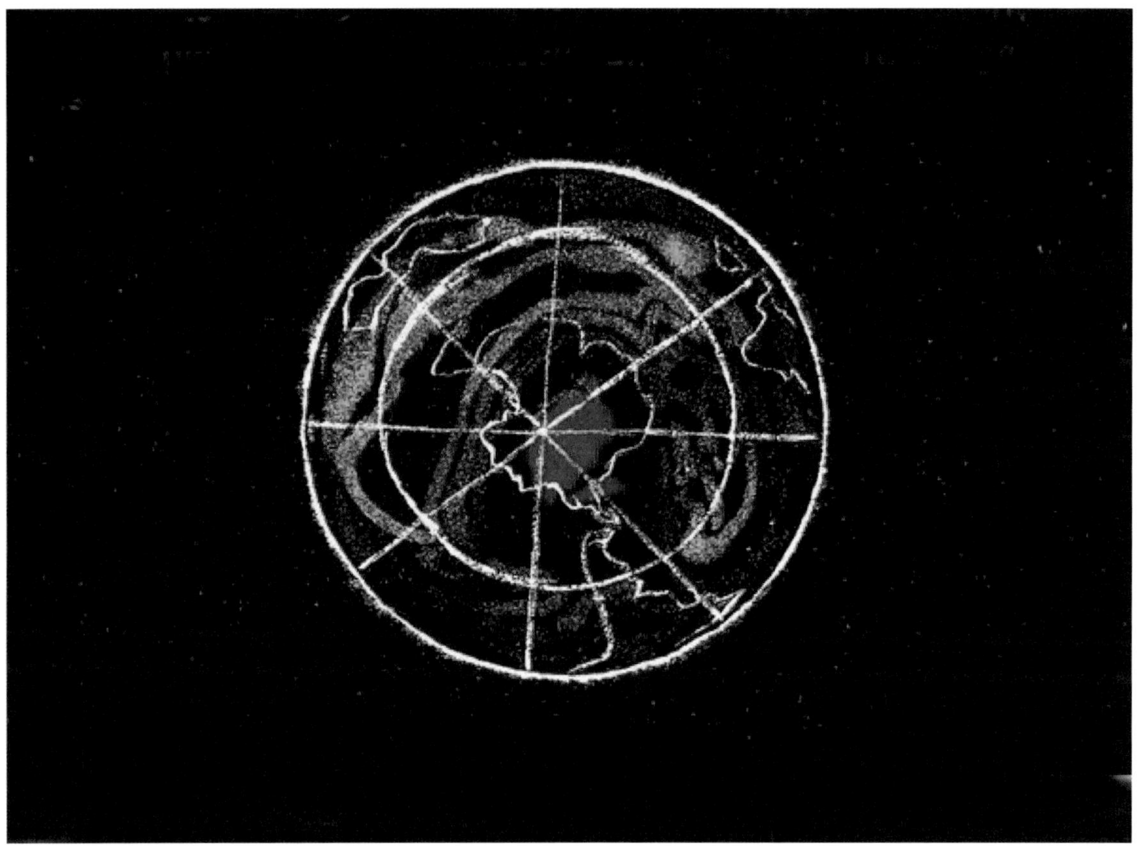

The Ozone-hole in the upper stratosphere meant that more people got skin cancer.

In this satellite image it is seen as a red spot.

Now the Ozone-hole is closed again because the bad chemicals in the old hairsprays and refrigerators were forbidden.

This proves to us that action on climate change can work!

Mankind has a responsibility that Allah has given us. In the Surah Ar-Rahman Allah describes the beauty of nature and then says:

"And the heaven He raised and imposed the balance, So that you do not disturb the balance.

And establish weight with justice and do not transgress the balance."

Surah Ar-Rahman55, Ayah 7-8

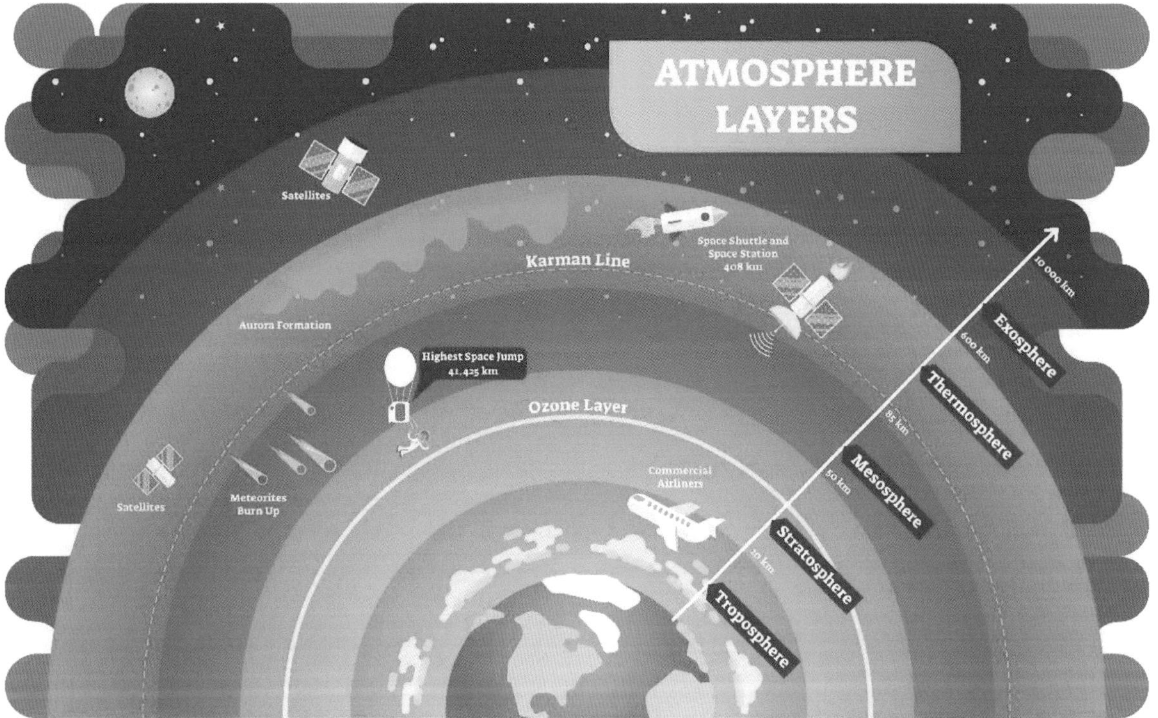

Allah swears an oath on the atmosphere "By the atmosphere which reflects (sends back)..."
Surah At-Tariq, 86 Ayah 11

All the layers of the atmosphere reflect something back out into the universe or back down to Earth. They protect the Earth from loss of air so we can breathe and like the ozonosphere (ozone layer) they protect us from danger. The ozone layer saves us from too much UV-light from the sun.

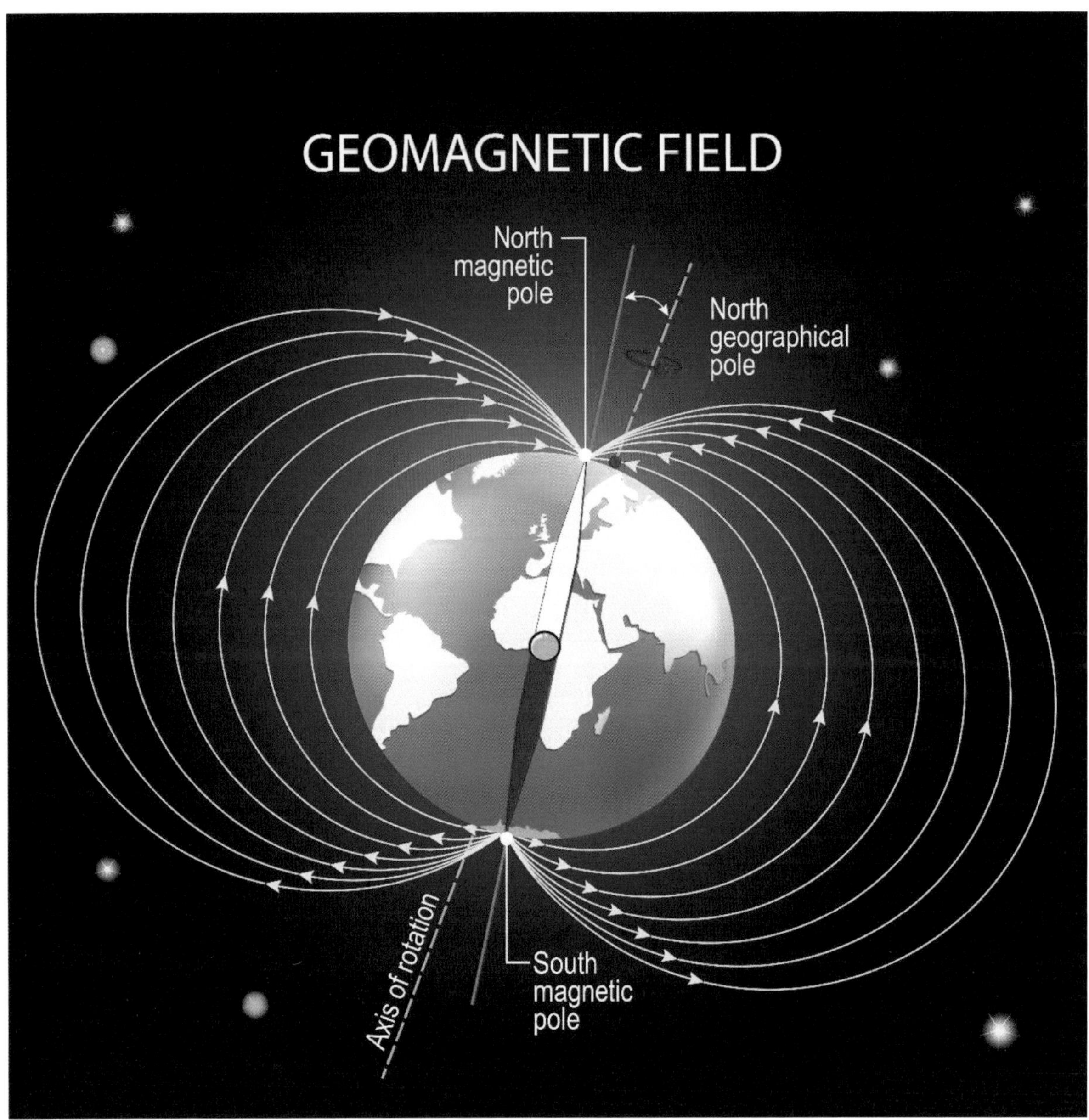

The Earth's magnetic shield, the magnetosphere, reflects tiny hazardous particles back into the universe.

The Thermosphere keeps the heat from the sun trapped so we can survive and not freeze.

The Troposphere keeps important gasses trapped down at our nearby areas so we can breathe.

All atmospheric layers play an important role, just like Allah says in Surah Ha-Mim, 41 Ayah 12. You can read it on the previous page.

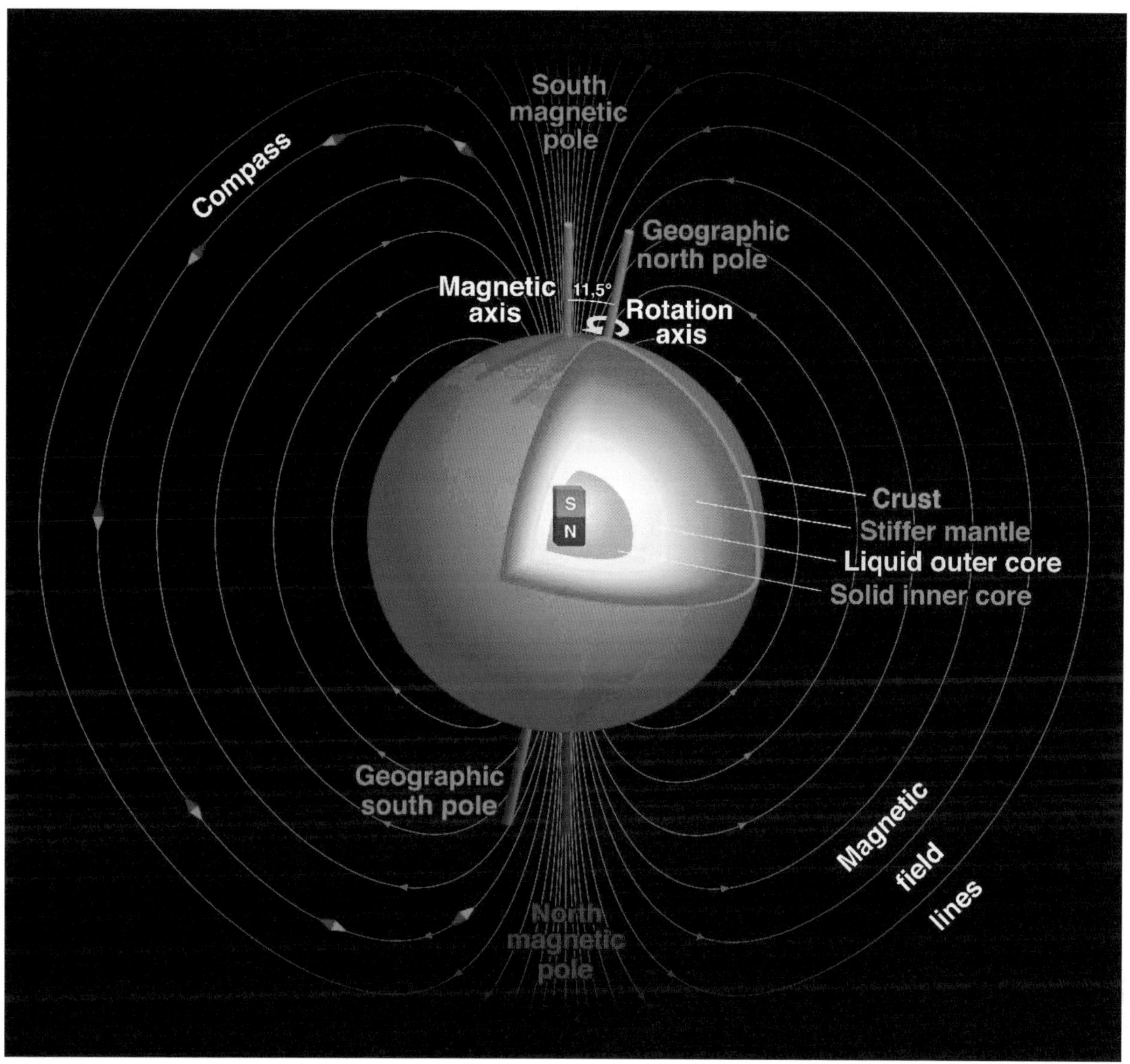

Allah also says in the Quran:

"Allah created seven atmospheres and of the Earth a similar number."

Surah At-Talaq 65, Ayah 12

With this Allah means the seven layers inside the Earth, which were unknown until scientists measured earthquakes. For this they used seismographs which were only invented by the middle of the 20th century, But the Quran is 1400 years old...

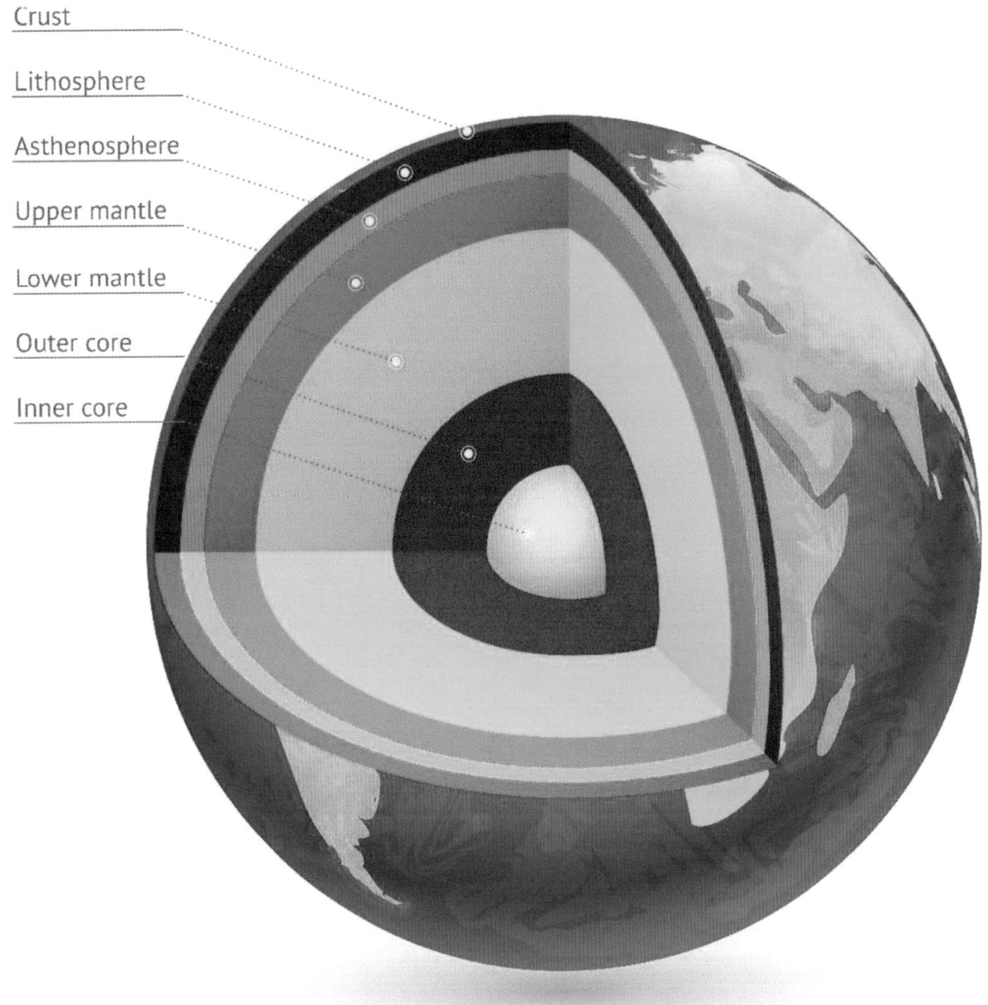

The seven inner layers of the Earth

1. Outer Crust
2. Inner Crust
3. Outer Mantle
4. Middle Mantle
5. Inner Mantle
6. Outer Core
7. Inner Core

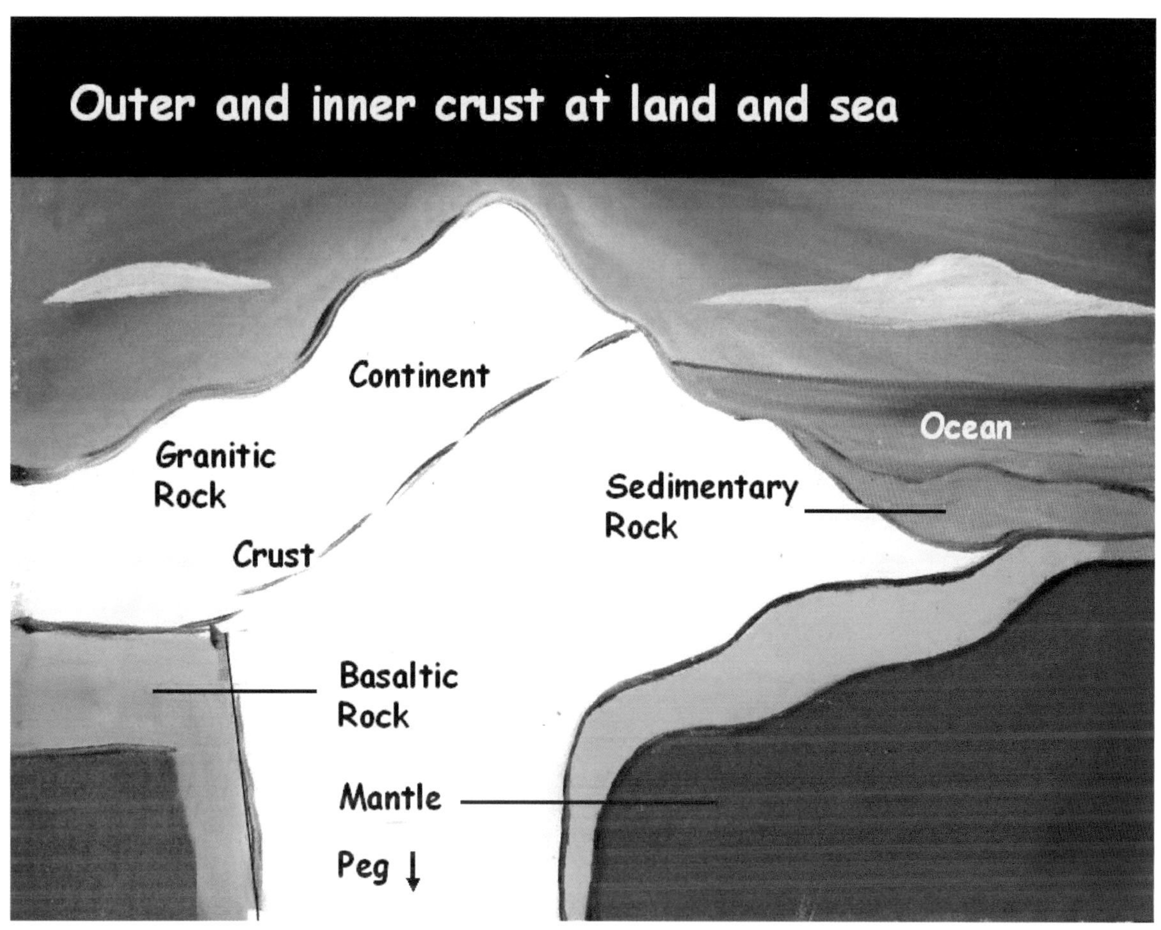

Outer and inner crust at land and sea:

Continent
Ocean
Granitic Rock or
Sedimentary Rock
Crust
Basaltic Rock
Mantle
Peg

This is a continental fault in California.
Here two continental plateaus meet each other.

Allah swears by the Earth in the Quran:

"By the Earth which is cracked"
12 Surah At-Tariq, 86 Ayah

The crust of the Earth is torn apart into many pieces which are called the continental plateaus.

They swim or drift on the liquid mantle which is like molten rock.

This is why the continents shift and the surface of the Earth changes. Mountains form and grow when plateaus push against each other...

Mountains are rich in minerals because they bring out rare materials from the Earth's interior.

"And He placed on the earth firm mountains, standing high, showered His blessings upon it, and ordained ⌜all⌝ its means of sustenance…"

Surah Ha-Mim 41, Ayah 10

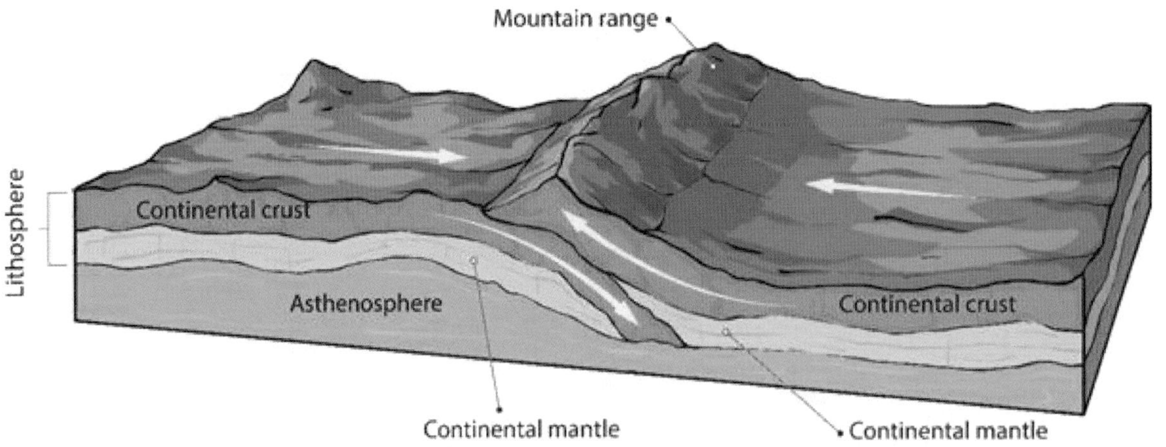

About the mountains Allah asks:

"And (did I not create) the mountains as pegs?" Surah An-Nabaa, 78 Ayah 7

Because of the continental drift the mountains are folded deep into the Earth and nail the crust into the mantle as shown on above.

Allah said 1400 years ago that they move, nevertheless. Scientists have only found this now. So, the last word of Allah, the Quran, is the truth.

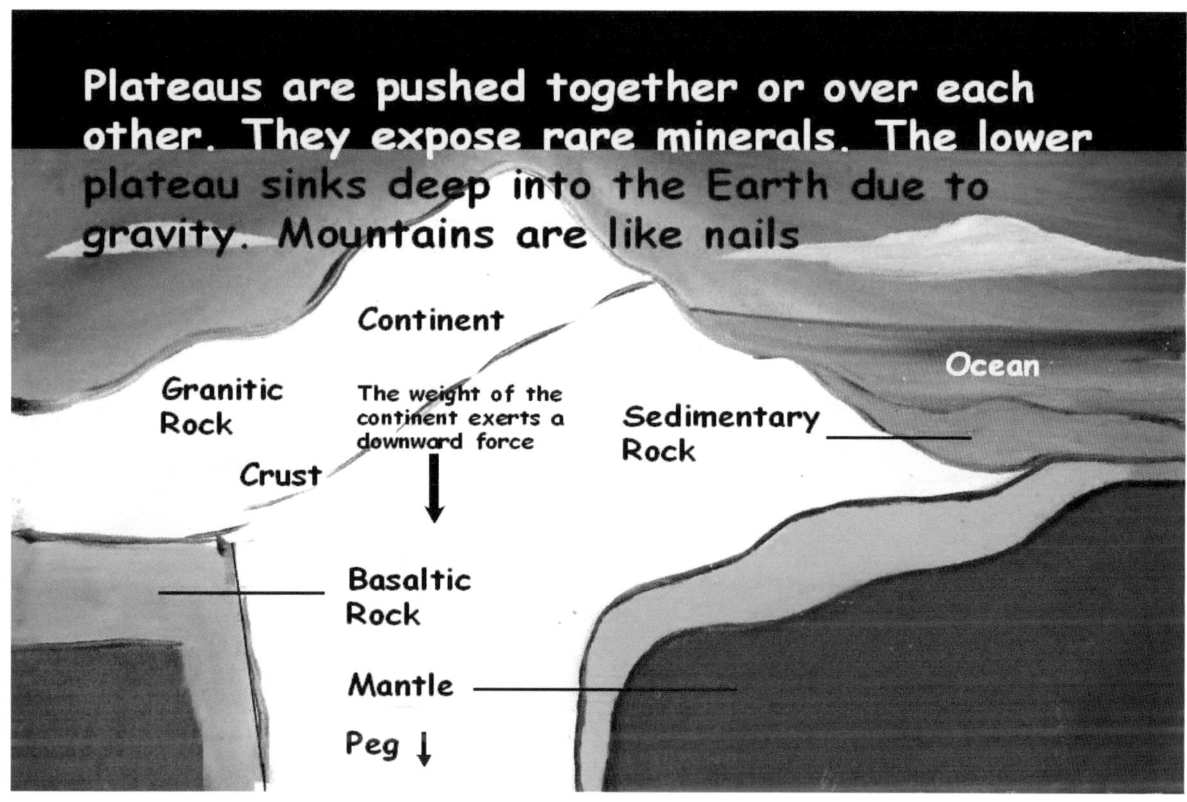

Plateaus are pushed together or over each other. They expose rare minerals. The lower plateau sinks deep into the Earth due to gravity. Mountains are like pegs or nails.

Continent

Ocean

Granitic Rock/Sedimentary Rock

Crust

Basaltic Rock

Mantle

Peg

The weight of the continent exerts a downward force.

The mountains move with the plateaus and fold to form caves:

"You see the mountains and you think they are firmly fixed but they pass away like clouds pass away"
Surah An-Naml 27, Ayah 88

Summary 1

In the Quran Allah has revealed exact details about the seven layers of the Earth's atmosphere, it's seven interior layers and the mountains.

There are details about the protective duty of the atmosphere and the fact that it reflects many things, all these are signs from Allah.

There are also verses about the seven interior layers of the Earth. Also, the movement of the crust and the formation of the mountains is in the Quran.

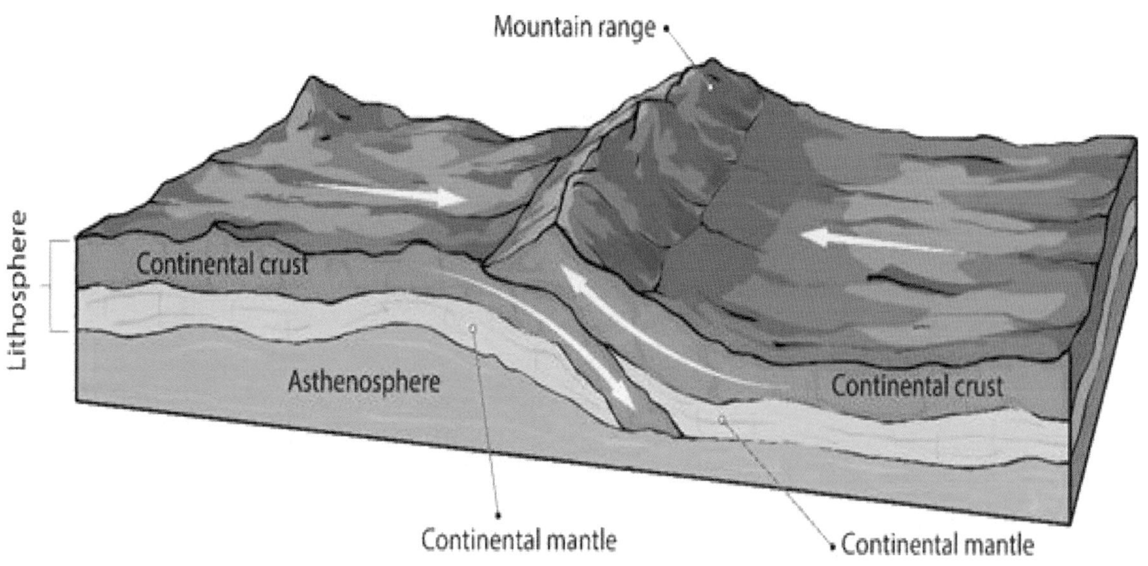

Summary 2

The Quran also describes the fact that mountains are like pegs which stabilise the crust.

They are also important for us because they give us minerals, which Allah calls nourishment, because they are important for life.

These are scientific discoveries of the 20th century and have been proven to be true by seismographic measurements just last century.

Summary 3

The Quran was revealed to the Prophet Mohammed (peace be upon him) 1400 years ago at a time when seismographs, submarines and satellites did not exist.

Scientific discoveries in the areas of Astronomy, Geology and Biology are important for us because we are living in the Age of Science and technology.

All around us there are more and more inventions like cars, rockets and satellites. We must use these inventions to do good.

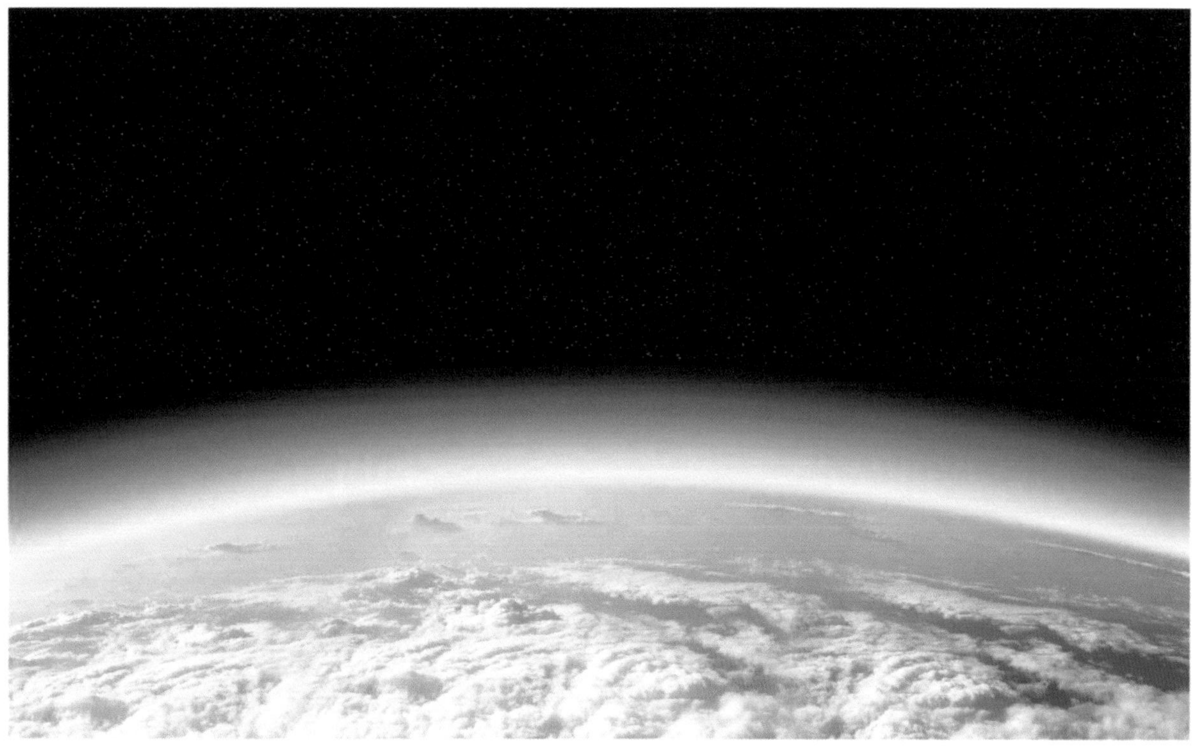

Summary 4

Someone who does not believe that science is true should not drive a car or even a bicycle.

Allah has given us special signs for every Age in his book, the Quran. He has also given us many scientific signs in all different areas of science.

The Quran is a revelation from Allah, the Creator These are only a few of Allah's signs. There are many more...

There is no God but Allah
And Mohammed is His Messenger

Part 4
Geology
Water

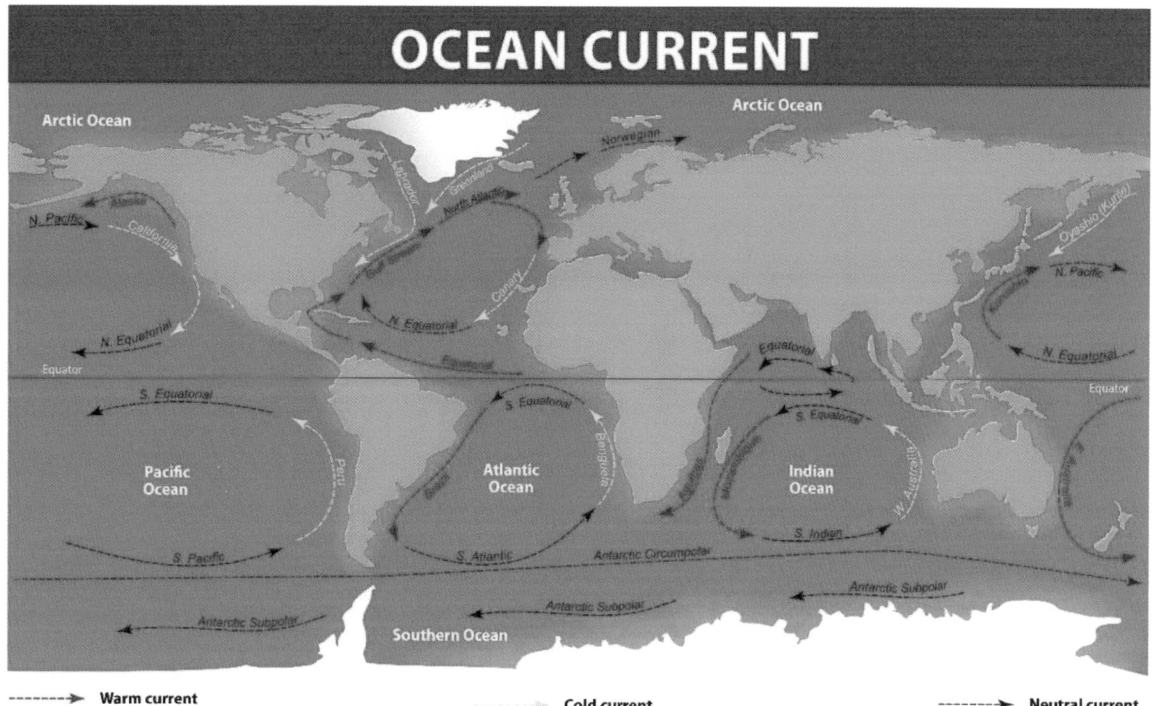

In the name of Allah, the Most Forgiving, Most Merciful.

In the Quran Allah said about himself 1400 years ago:

"It is He Who has let free the two bodies of flowing water: one palatable and sweet and the other salty and bitter; yet has He made a barrier between them a partition that is forbidden to be passed."

Surah Al-Furqan, 25 Ayah 53

From recent scientific discoveries we know today:

Sweet water in rivers and seas does not intermix easily with water in the oceans.

Brackish (mixed) water is part of the river estuary and could be classified as a boundary between sweet and salt water. Only brackish water has high and low tide like sea water, sweet water doesn't.

The barrier between sweet- and salt-water has a so-called osmotic gradient, where certain mineral pass only very slowly, generating a lot of energy.

This energy can be used in so-called Osmotic Generators to generate electricity in an environmentally friendly way.

It is a fact that...

...the Earth's water is constantly recycled. It falls on the land as rain and snow, is carried by rivers or groundwater to the oceans, rises as water vapor to form clouds, and travels inland again.

This process is called the…

Hydrological Cycle.

Without this cycle the rotting corpses of dead animals and plants would smell unbearably. We would not be able to breathe the air around us. Allah mentions the water cycle in the Quran as one of His Signs.

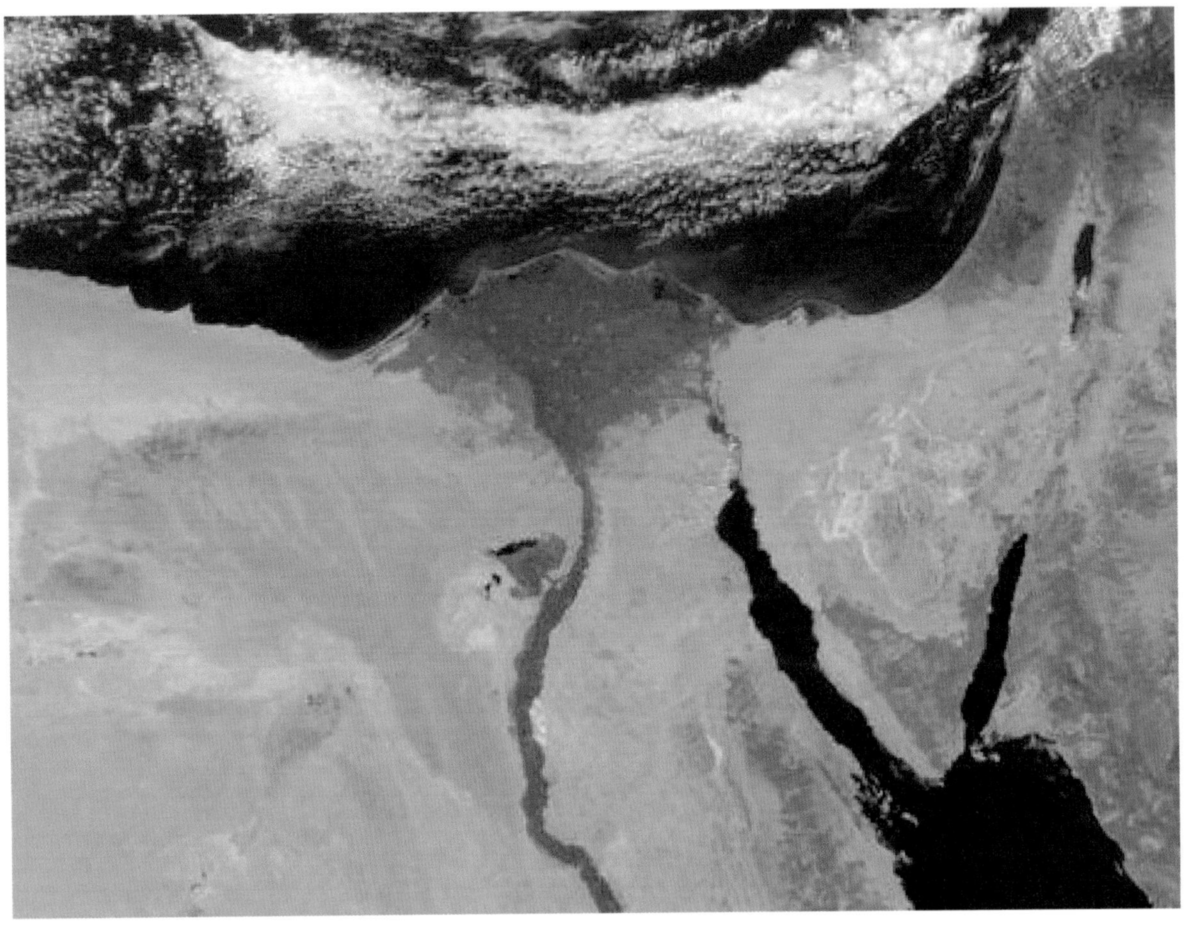

This is the river estuary of the Nile as seen from the air

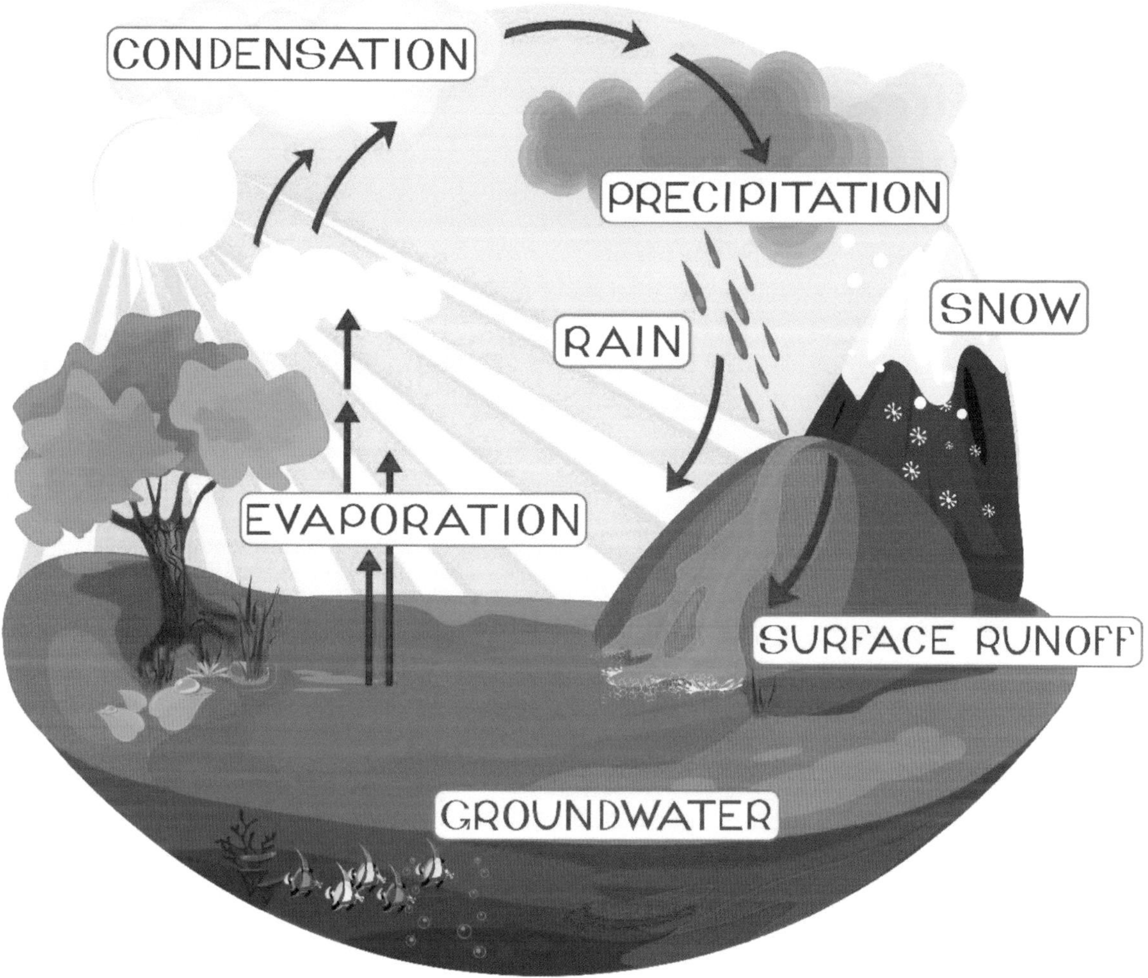

The Water Cycle:

- Condensation
- Snow
- Atmospheric Moisture
- Rain
- Evaporation
- Transpiration
- Glaciers
- Run off
- Streams
- Groundwater

Allah swears an oath in the Quran:

"And by the Ocean filled with fire"
Surah At-Tur, 52 Ayah 7

Scientists know now that volcanoes spit out fire under the ocean, which was not known at the time the Quran was sent 1400 years ago to Mohammed (peace be upon him).

However, there is even much more fire under the ocean! That is a discovery of the 1970s.

A volcano pours out lava into the sea

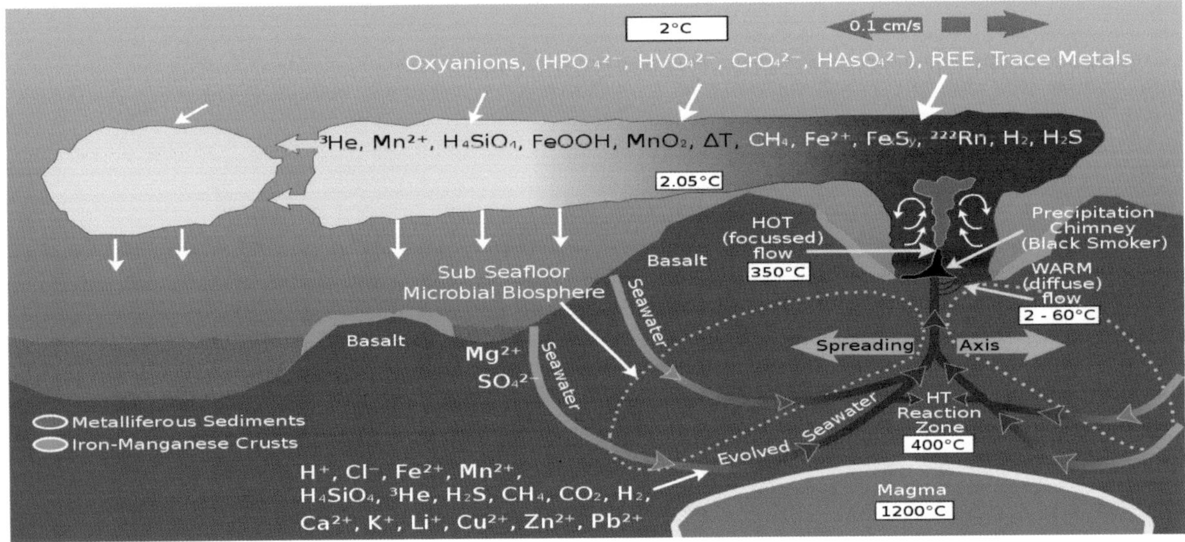

There is even more fire underneath the ocean

There is also smoke at the very bottom of the ocean coming out of black smokers or geothermal vents from the Earths interior.

Normally water extinguishes fire. Still here at the bottom of the ocean this doesn't happen. The fire is not hot enough to make the water evaporate (turn to steam), nor is the water cold enough to extinguish this fire. The smoke of this fire comes from the Earth's mantle and is full of minerals and nourishes a whole biosystem under the ocean which needs no sunlight (see book 5). This is a sign from Allah and a fine balance he has set up.

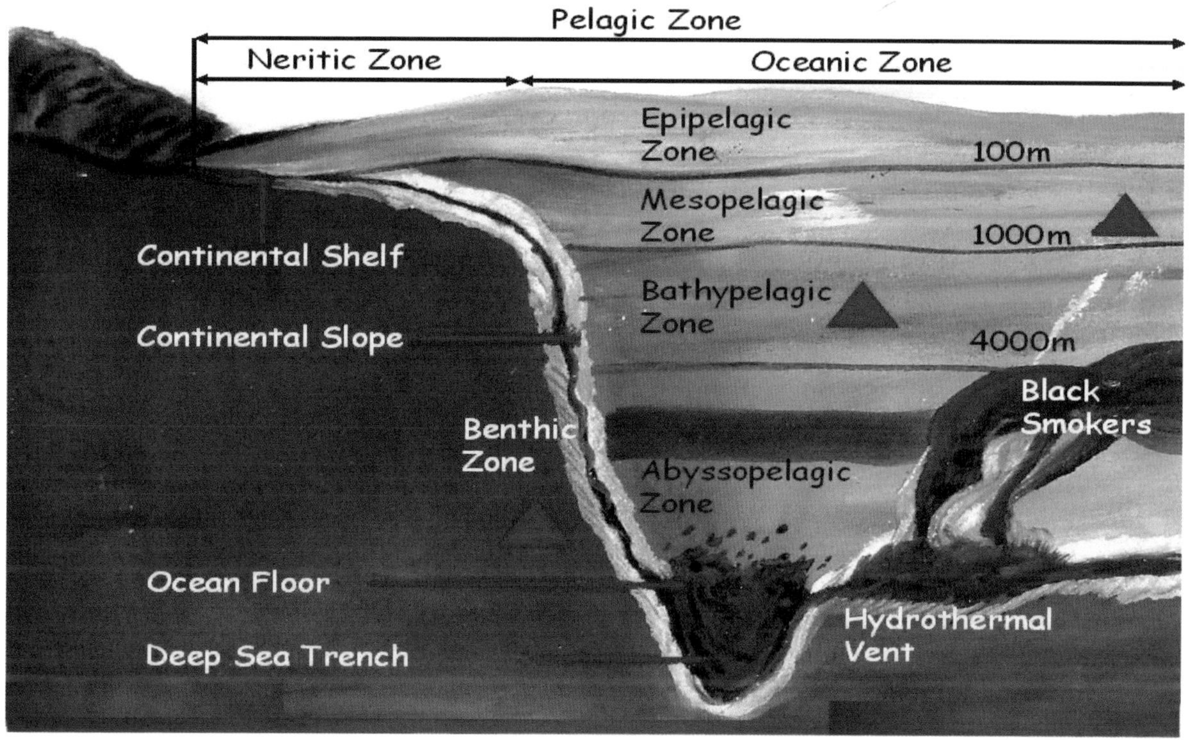

In this picture of the Ocean, you can see:

Pelagic Zone

Oceanic Zone

Neritic Zone

100m

Epipelagic Zone Mesopelagic Zone

1000m

Continental Shelf

Bathypelagic Zone

Continental Slope

4000m

Black Smokers

Benthic Zone

Abyssopelagic Zone

Ocean Floor

Hydrothermal Vent

Deep Sea Trench

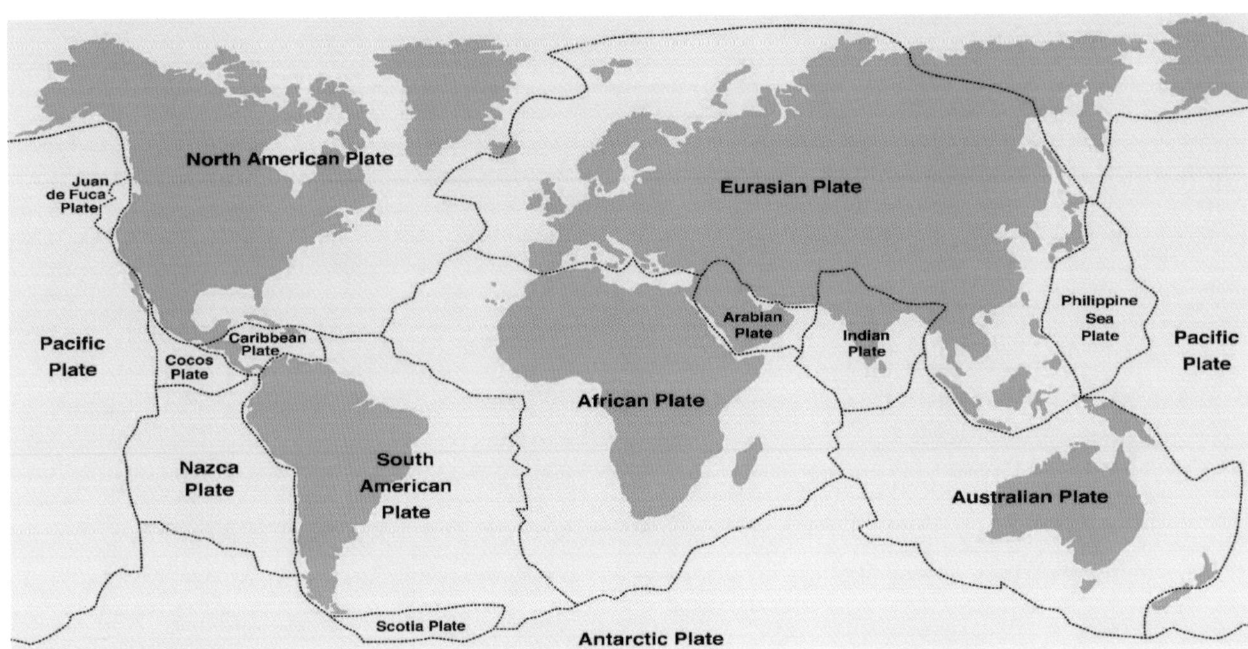

Allah swears another oath in the Quran

"By the Earth which is cracked"
Surah At-Tariq, 86 Ayah 12

Black smokers are mainly located along the cracks in the continental plateaus where they help the Earth's interior to "let off steam" so it does not explode.

They also serve the purpose of providing important minerals to the water and that is why Allah points at their importance in two oaths, by the ocean filled with fire and by the Earth which is cracked. Allah knows all of creation, even the bottom of the oceans and the cracks in between the continents since he created it all.

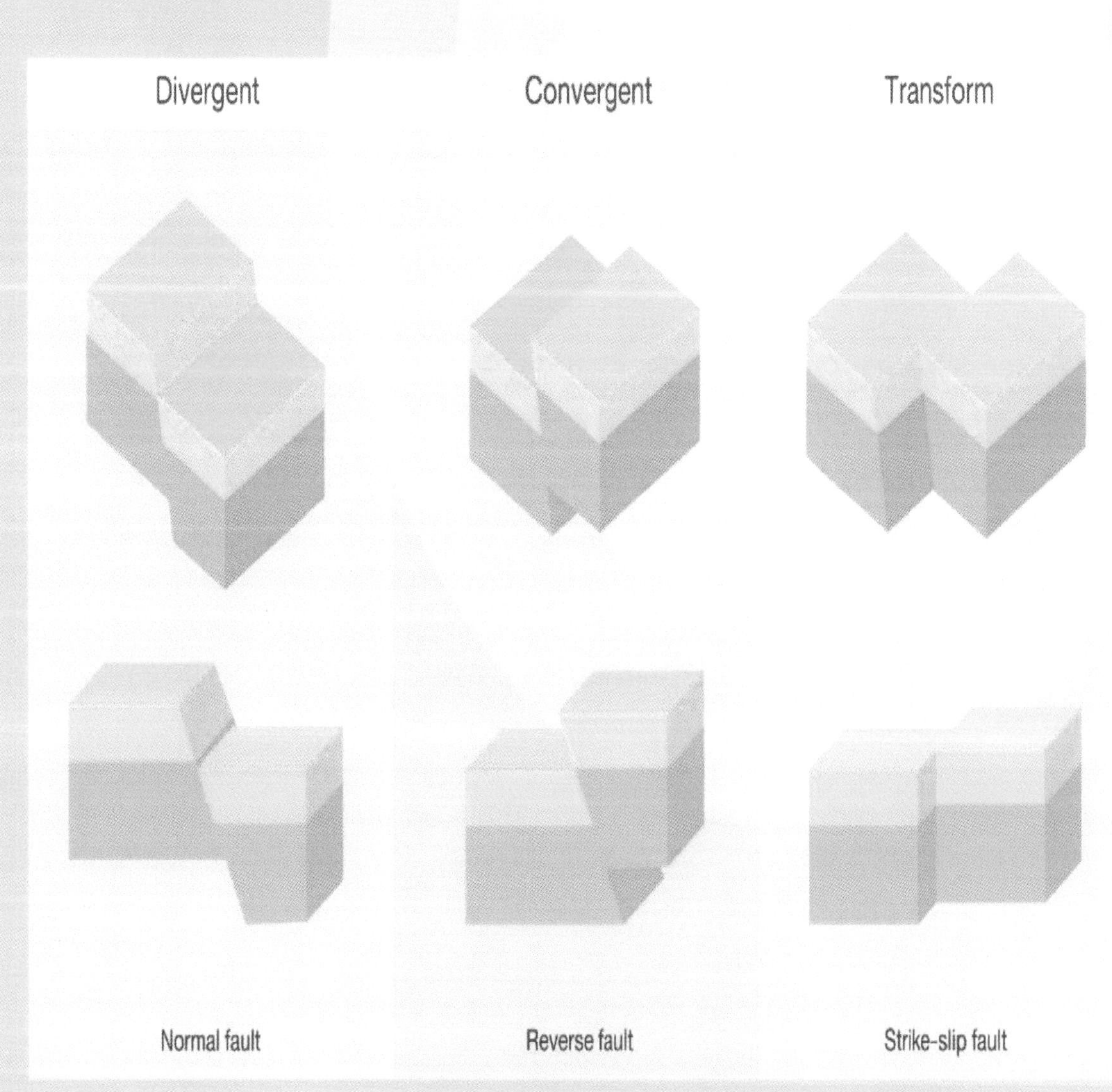
TYPES OF PLATE BOUNDARY
Divergent
Convergent
Transform
Normal fault
Reverse fault
Strike-slip fault

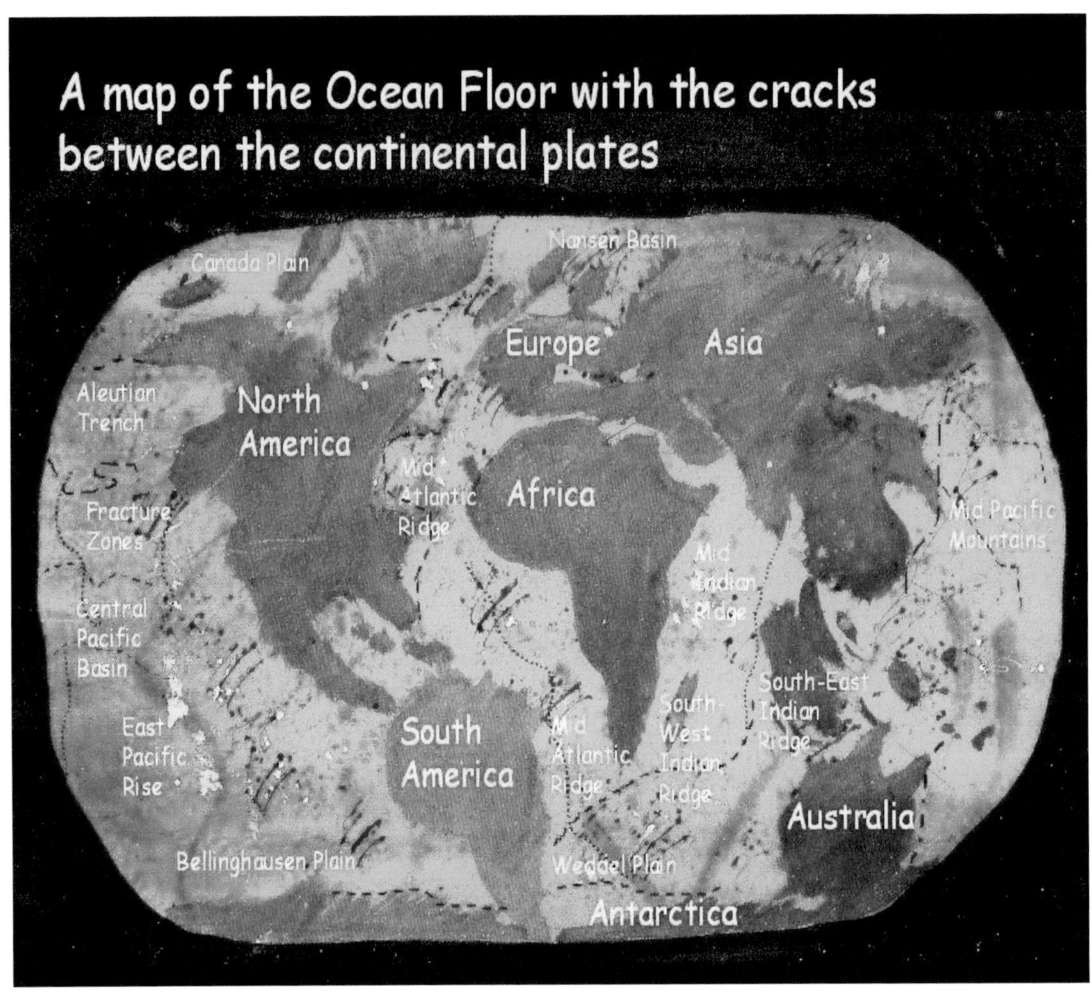

A map of the Ocean with cracks between the continental plates:

The continents: Europe, Asia, Africa, North America, South America, Australia and Antarctica

The basins: Nansen Basin, Central Pacific Basin

The plains: Canada Plain, Bellingshausen Plain, Weddell Plain

The trenches: Aleutian Trench

The ridges: Mid Atlantic Ridge, Mid Indian Ridge, South-East Indian Ridge, Southwest Indian Ridge

Mid Pacific Mountains and East Pacific Rise

Fracture Zones across all oceans

Allah also says in the Quran

" The state of one who rejects is like the depths of darkness in a vast deep ocean overwhelmed with waves topped by waves topped by (dark) clouds: depths of darkness one above another: if a man stretches out his hand he can hardly see it!"

Surah An-Nur, 24 Ayah 40

In this verse Allah describes exactly how he has layered cold and warm water waves above each other. They flow in a complex pattern in all oceans as discovered recently.

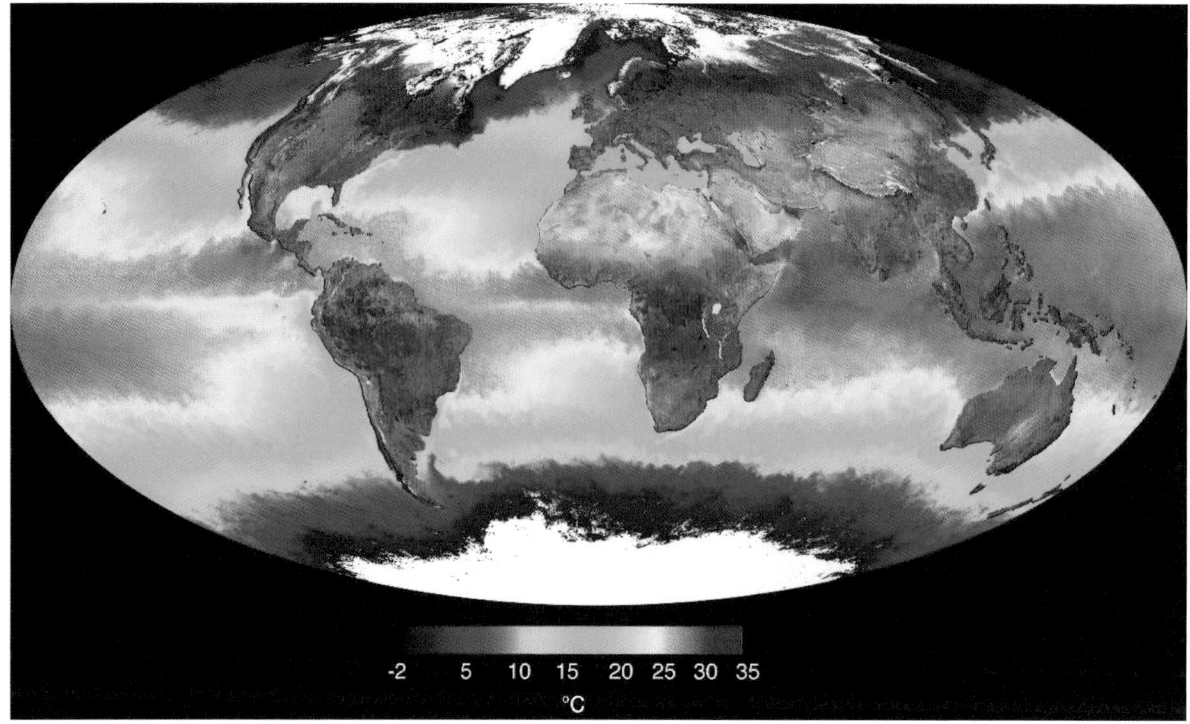

Satellite images show the depth of the oceans and their temperature. Deep water is close to land and shallow water actually far away from it.

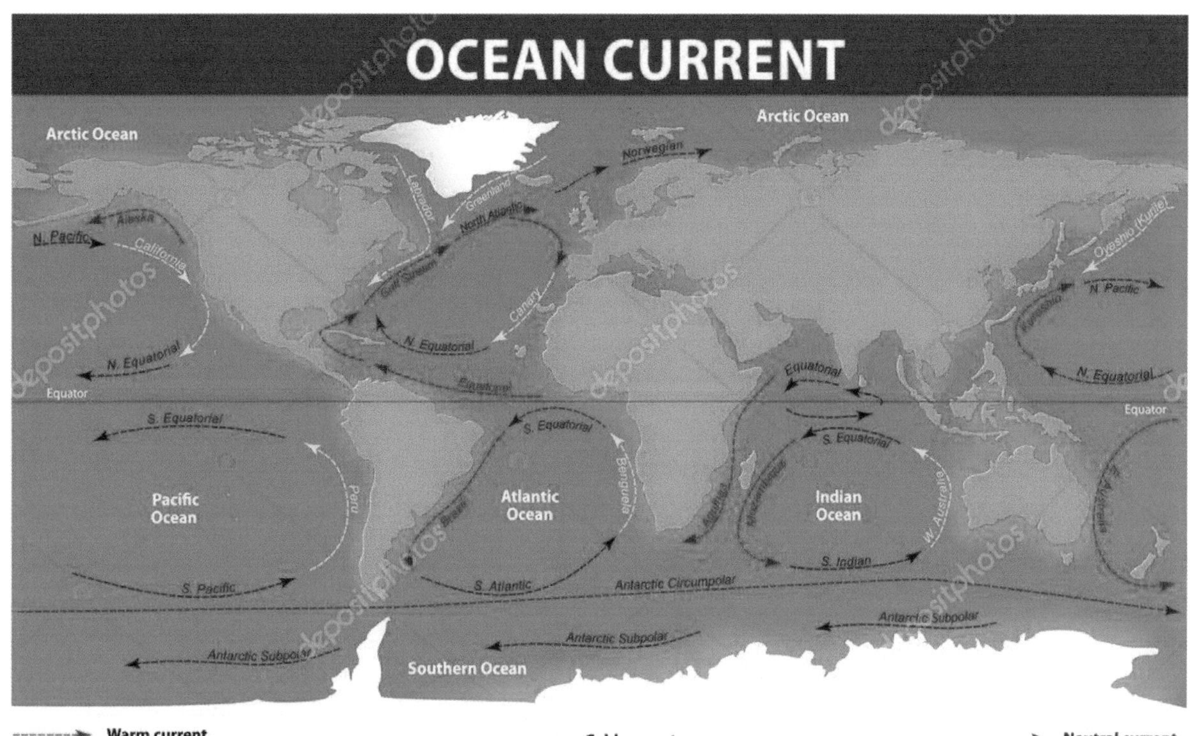
OCEAN CURRENT
Arctic Ocean
Arctic Ocean
Norwegian
Labrador
Greenland
North Atlantic
Alaska
N. Pacific
California
Gulf Stream
Canary
N. Equatorial
N. Equatorial
Equatorial
Equator
S. Equatorial
Pacific Ocean
Peru
S. Pacific
Antarctic Subpolar
S. Equatorial
Atlantic Ocean
Benguela
S. Atlantic
Antarctic Circumpolar
Antarctic Subpolar
Southern Ocean
Equatorial
S. Equatorial
Indian Ocean
W. Australia
S. Indian
Antarctic Subpolar
Oyashio (Kurile)
N. Pacific
N. Equatorial
Equator
Warm current
Cold current
Neutral current

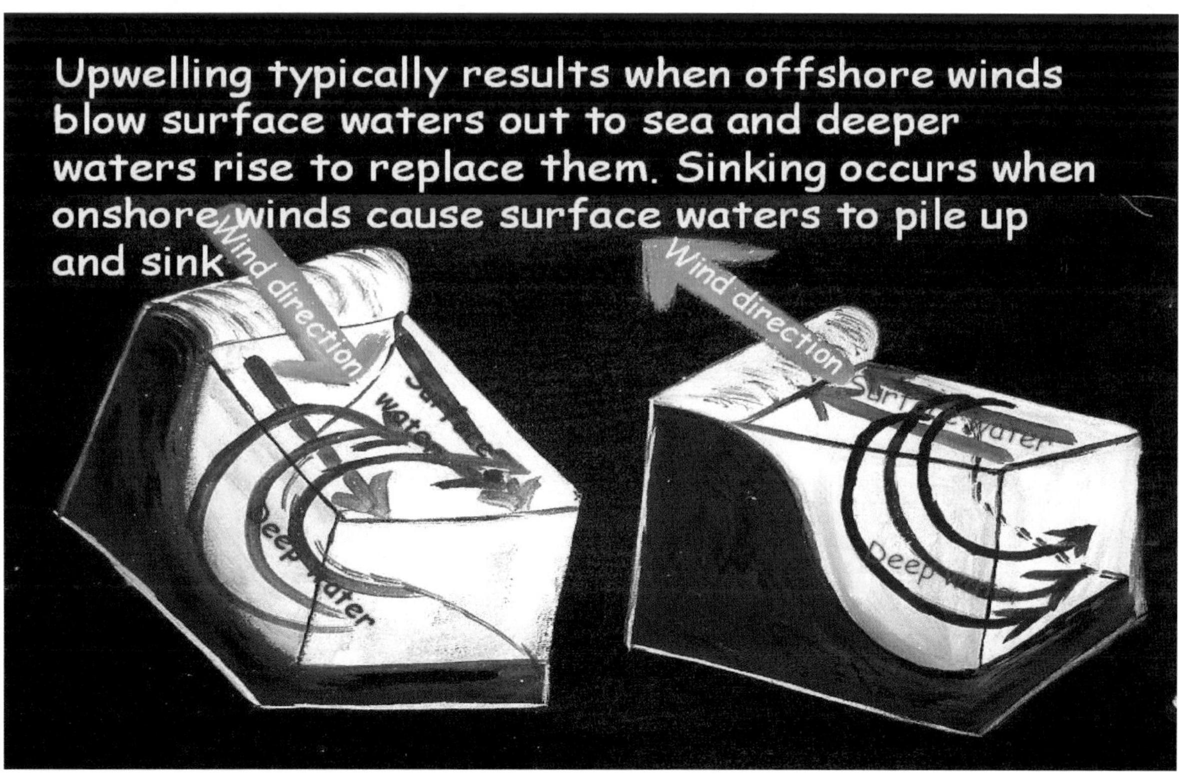
Upwelling typically results when offshore winds blow surface waters out to sea and deeper waters rise to replace them. Sinking occurs when onshore winds cause surface waters to pile up and sink
Wind direction
Wind direction

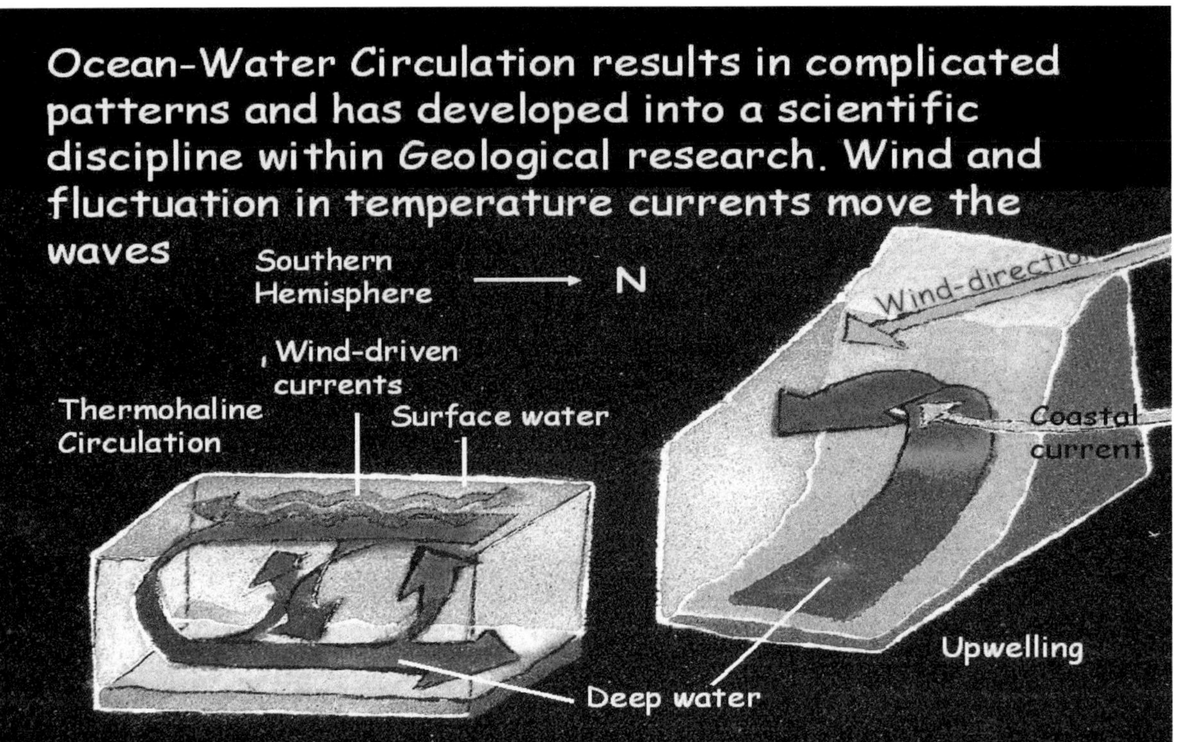
Ocean-Water Circulation results in complicated patterns and has developed into a scientific discipline within Geological research. Wind and fluctuation in temperature currents move the waves
Southern Hemisphere
N
Wind-driven currents
Thermohaline Circulation
Surface water
Deep water
Upwelling
Coastal current
Wind-directio

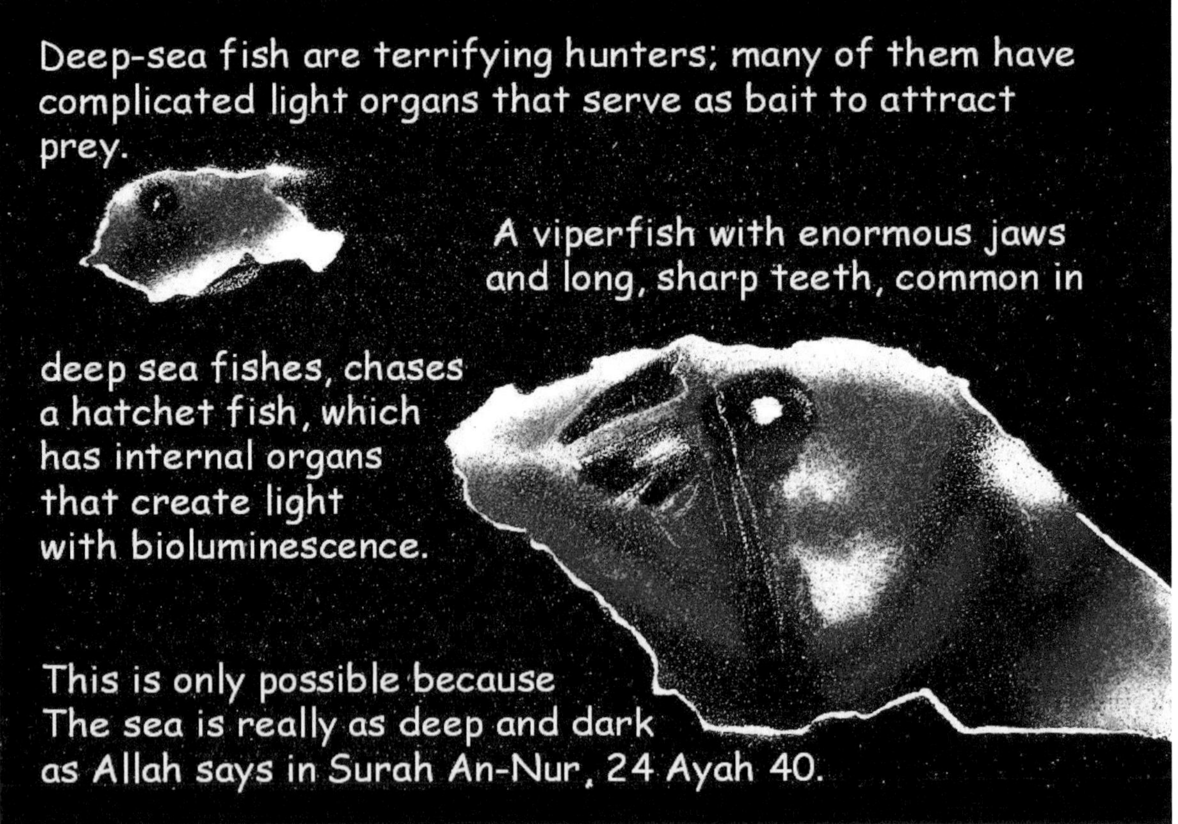
Deep-sea fish are terrifying hunters; many of them have complicated light organs that serve as bait to attract prey.
A viperfish with enormous jaws and long, sharp teeth, common in deep sea fishes, chases a hatchet fish, which has internal organs that create light with bioluminescence.
This is only possible because The sea is really as deep and dark as Allah says in Surah An-Nur, 24 Ayah 40.

Allah promises in the Quran:

"Soon will We show them Our Signs in the (distant) regions and in their own souls until it becomes manifest to them that this (the Koran) is the Truth. Is it not enough that thy Lord doth witness all things?"

Surah Ha-Mim, 41 Ayah 53

In this Ayah Allah promises us that he will show us his signs clearly in all areas of Astronomy, Geology and Biology. We have seen signs in Astronomy in book 1 and 2 of this series. We have also seen Geology in book 3 and 4, which is this one. We will continue with Biology in book 5 and 6. But before another important Ayah (verse).

Allah also says about himself and his creation in the Quran:

"He who created the seven heavens one above another; no lack of proportion will you see in the Creation of (Allah) Most Gracious so turn your vision again: Do you see any mistake? Again, turn your vision a second time; your vision will come back to you dull and, in a state, worn out."
Surah Al-Mulk, 67 Ayah 3, 4

Allah reminds us of the perfection of His creation and asks us to check it again and again. He commands us to observe his creation as much as possible.

Summary 1

In the Quran Allah has revealed exact details about the water cycle, rivers, and the ocean, which are his creation.

There are details about the water cycle, the way sweet water is separated from salt water, and the fact that there is fire at the bottom of the ocean along the continental faults. All these are Allah's signs.

There are also verses about the way the oceanic waves are structured, the complicated pattern of warm and cold water flowing into each other and the fact that the bottom of the ocean is completely dark.

Summary 2

These are scientific discoveries of the 20th century and have been proven to be true by using submarines and modern measurement less than 20-30 years ago. The Quran was revealed to the Prophet Mohammed (peace be upon him) 1400 years ago at a time when submarines and satellites did not exist. The Quran covers many aspects of modern science.

The Quran is a revelation from Allah, the Creator. These are only a few of Allah's signs. There are many more…

There is no God but Allah
And Mohammed is His Messenger

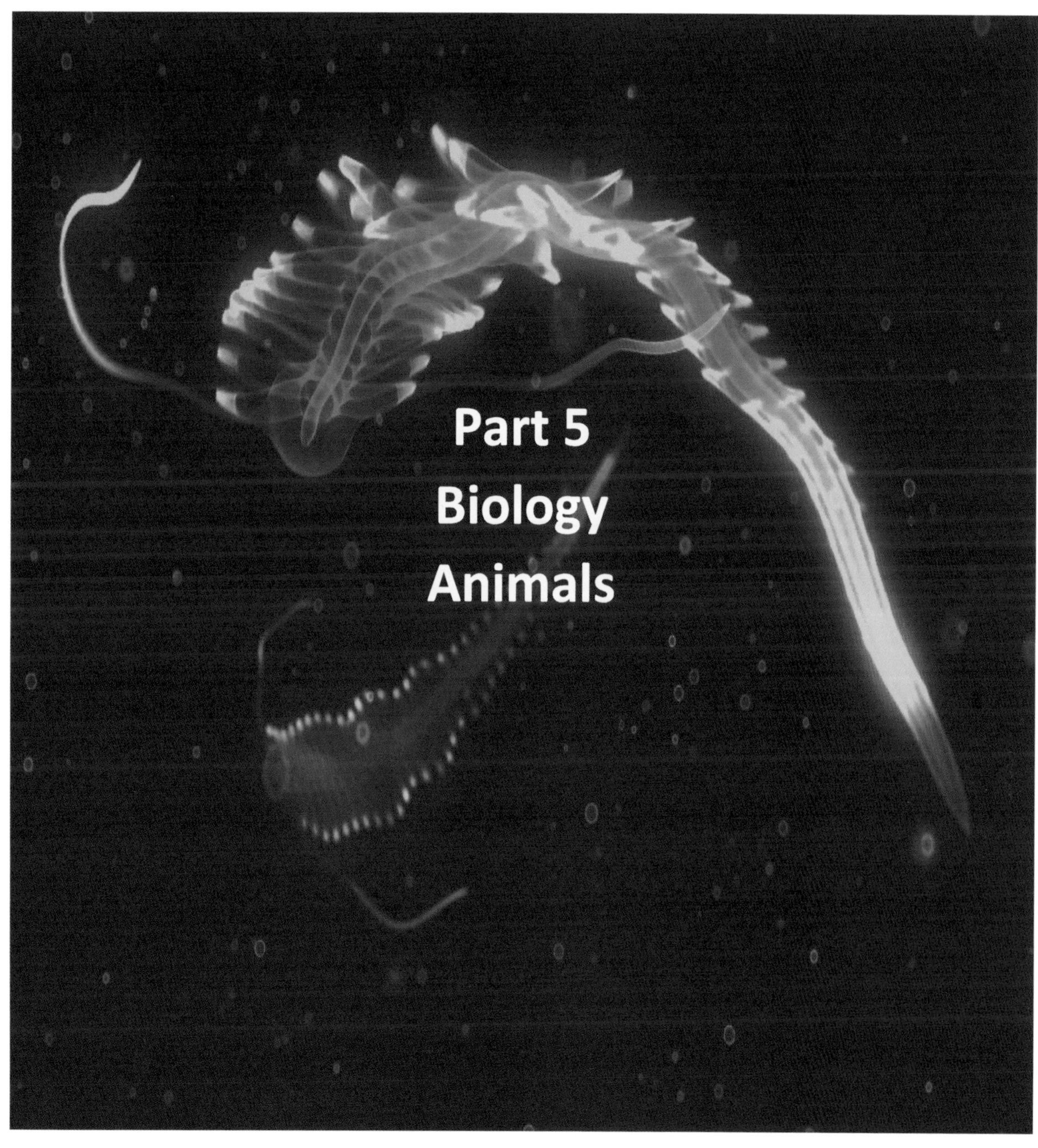
Part 5
Biology
Animals

In the name of Allah, the Most Forgiving, Most Merciful.

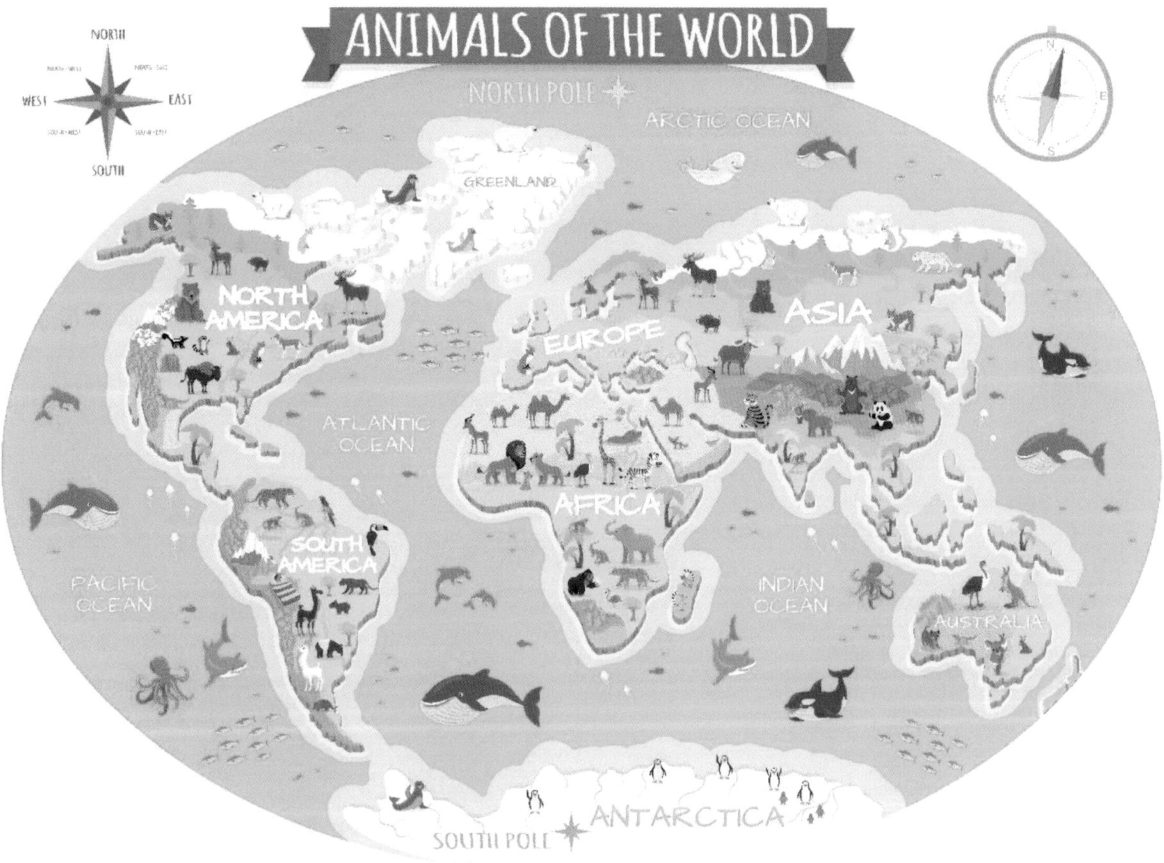

In the Quran Allah commands us to... "... Travel through the Earth and see how Allah brought forth creation..."
Surah Al Ankabut, 29 Ayah 20

If we believe in Allah, we must follow his command. Like this we can understand the world and be better people. We will also fight less with each other because we will understand the true religion and follow its rules which command peace.

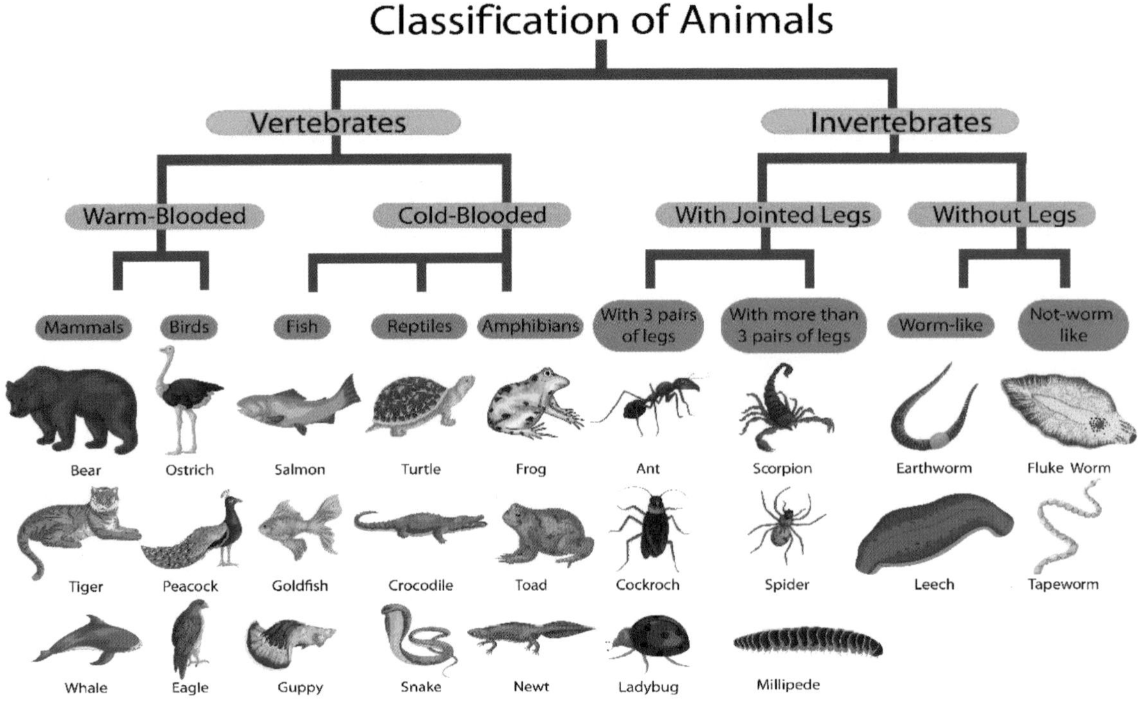

In the Quran Allah said about himself 1400 years ago:

"He is Allah the Creator, the Changer, the Former of shapes and colours. To Him belong the Most Beautiful Names..." Surah Al-Hashr, 59 Ayah 24

Allah has 99 names, and these are 3 of them. This indicates that Allah created life and then changed it after he had created it. He keeps shaping animals, plants, humans, and their environment. Scientists call this evolution. Evolution is the same as creation, but most people don't understand. Scientists and religious people both can be ignorant sometimes

Allah also says:

"He [Moses] said [to Pharaoh]: 'Our Cherisher (Allah) is He who created everything and then directed it."
Surah Ta Ha, 20 Ayah 50

This means that Allah created everything and then changed it with a clear purpose and aim, not just randomly. Most scientists believe that evolution has happened without any intention and that there is no God who has made it happen. They believe in so called random mutation and selection trough survival of the fittest. But in fact, Allah selects who survives. He changes the climate and other environmental circumstances intentionally. Allah also changes the beings and their genes (mutation).

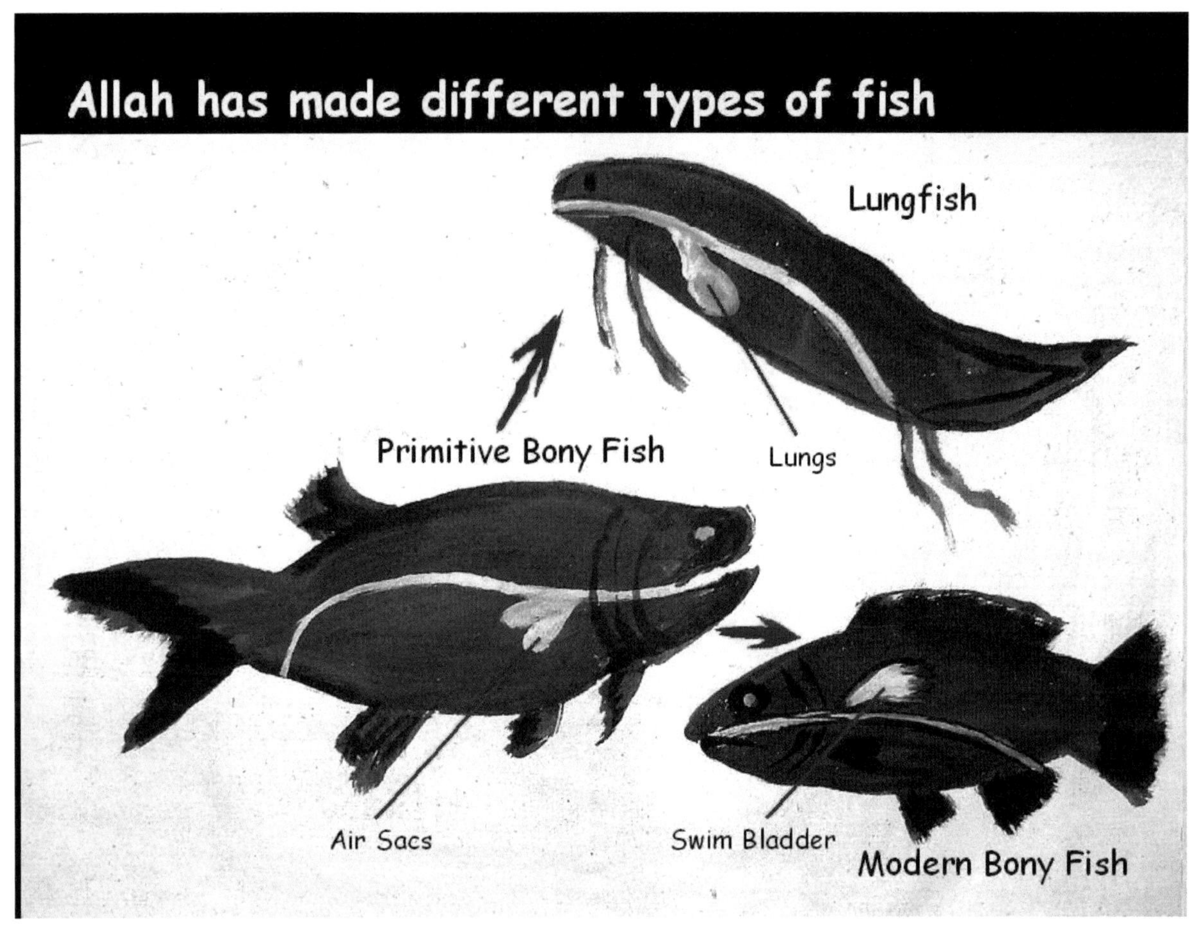

Allah has made different types of fish:

Lungfish

Primitive Bony Fish Modern Bony Fish

They have:

Lungs

Air Sacs

Swim Bladders

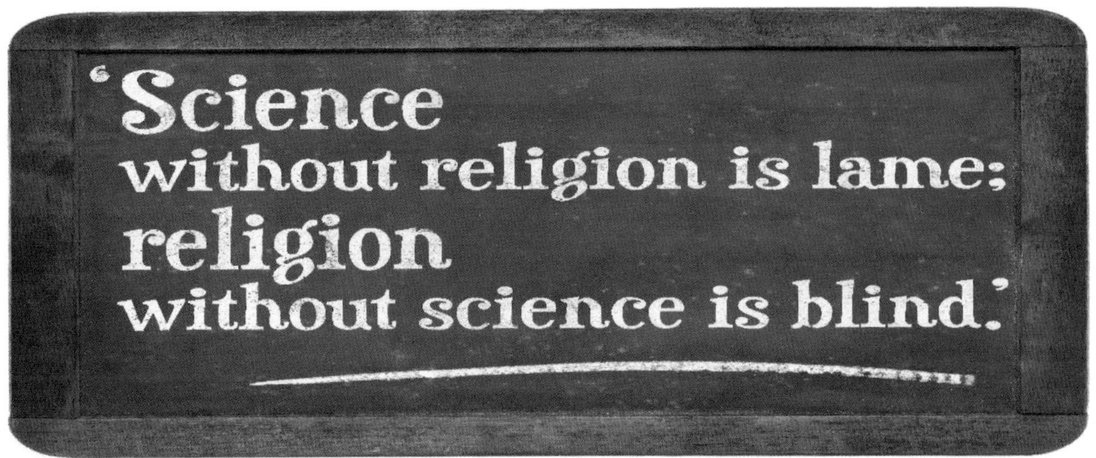

But people...

Many religious people do not believe in Evolution at all, although Allah says in the Quran that it has happened and there are clear proofs for it.

Many religious scholars or teachers try to convince people that science is wrong. That is why many scientists think religion is wrong.

This is the Age of Science and Technology. Allah has sent us his signs in the Quran for our Age so we can stay on the right path with confidence and certainty and practice the true religion, which is Islam.

The Bible has no scientific signs because it is too old for that. It is not the right book for our time!

Islam is the truth

Islam is a religion that explains evolution. It is a very scientific and modern religion. Muslims have made many important discoveries and inventions in the past. Even many Muslims don't know that. Islam is the truth, because in a book as old as the Quran there cannot be so many details about nature without any of them being wrong, unless it is from the One who knows everything, Allah, the Almighty, the Exalted.

And Allah has created...

"...Allah created every animal from water: of them there are some that creep on their bellies; some that walk on two legs; and some that walk on four. Allah creates what He wills: for verily Allah has power over all things."

Surah An-Nur, 24 Ayah 45

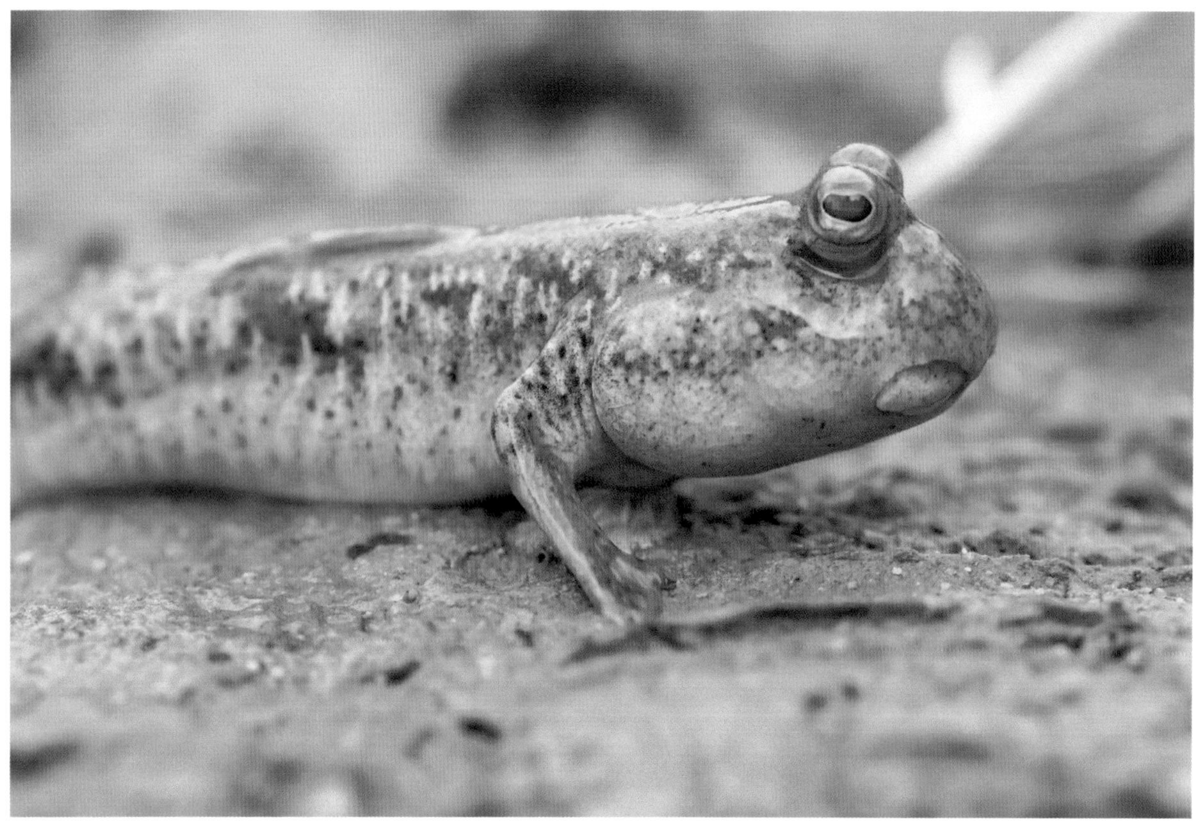

Allah has created fish that can walk on land (mudskippers)

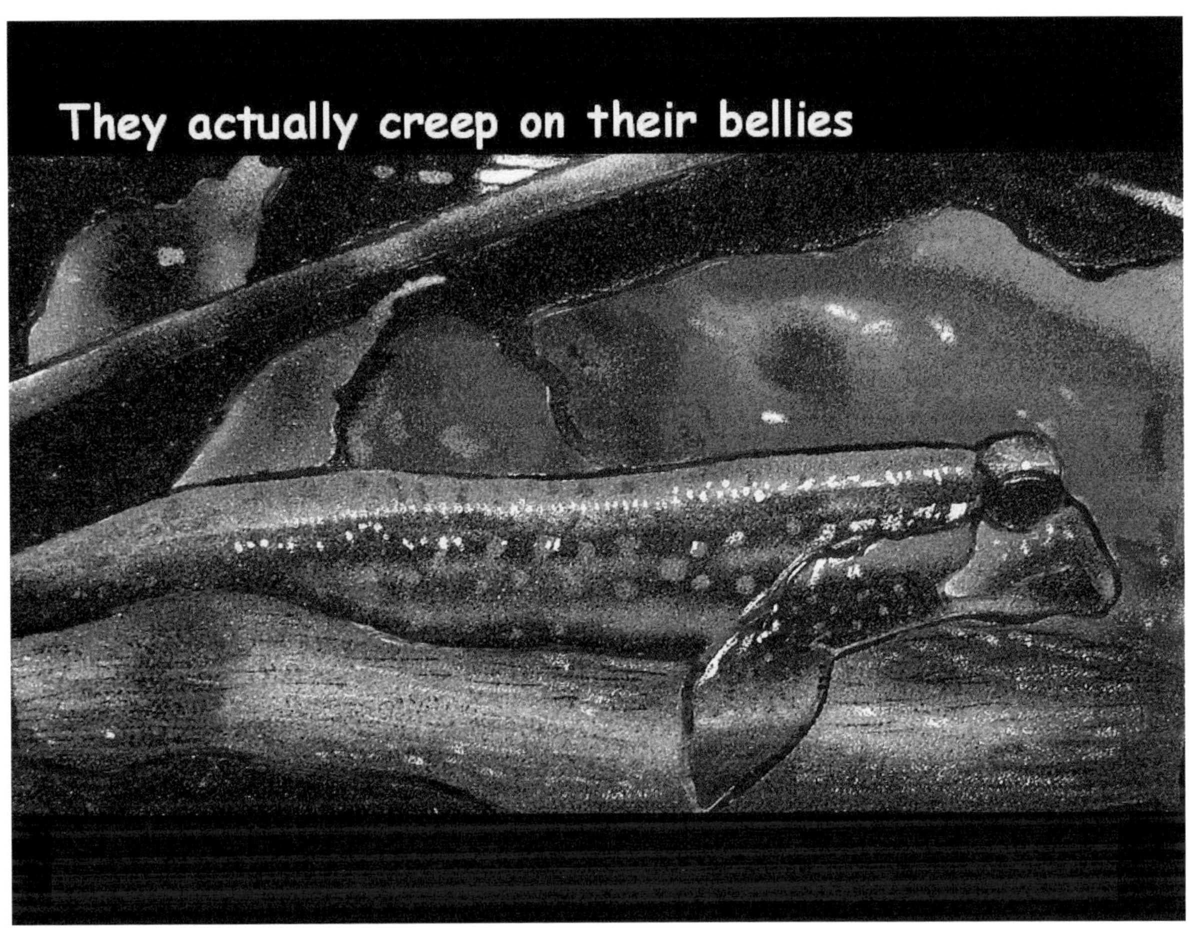
They actually creep on their bellies

Other fish can fly, as you can see on a previous page.

In the Quran a day (epoch or period) has different meanings:

"... a day the space of which will be (as) a thousand years for you." Surah As-Sajda, 32 Ayah 5

"...a day in the sight of your Lord is like a thousand years for you. Surah Al-Hajj, 22 Ayah 47

"... a day the measure whereof is (as) fifty thousand years..." Surah Al-Ma'arij, 70 Ayah 4

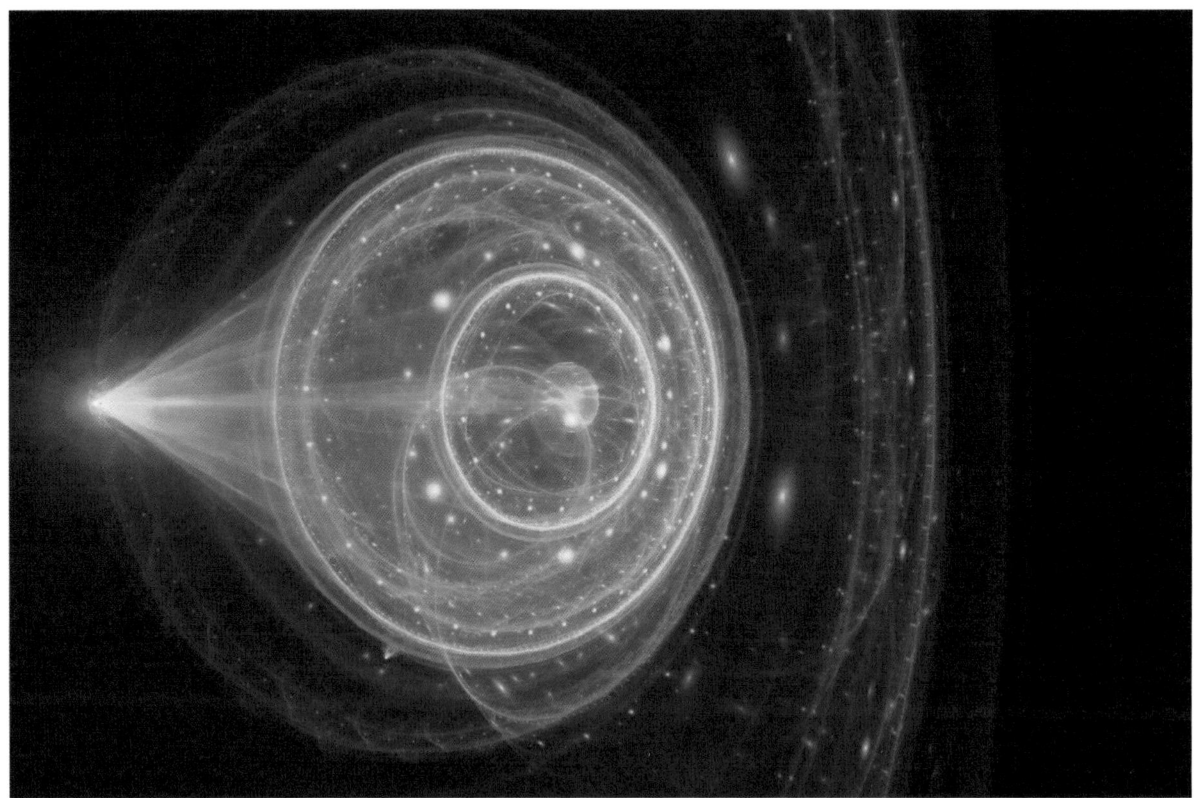

Allah says

"I created the Heavens and the Earth and all between them in Six Days nor did any feeling of tiredness touch me."
Surah Qaf, 50 Ayah 38

(The Bible says that God was tired and rested! But in reality, Allah never rests.) Some religious people say that Allah was tired after six days. That is not true, as he says above. Allah never gets tired. He hears and sees us all the time.

"Say: Do you deny Him Who created the Earth in two Days? And do ye join equals with Him? He is the Lord of (all) the Worlds."

Surah Ha-Mim, 41 Ayah 9

The timetable of evolution

Day or Quranic Period	Scientific Era	Scientific Period	Epoch	Time in years	Type of Organisms
see page 15		Bottleneck/Extinction/ Great Flood, see book 6 →		100,000	Homo Sapiens/Modern Man/Noah's People
Friday afternoon		Quaternary	Pleistocene	2,500,000	Homo Genus/Human Beings/Adam's People
	Cenozoic	Tertiary	Pliocene	12,000,000	Grazing and Carnivorous Mammals
			Miocene	26,000,000	
			Oligocene	38,000,000	
			Eocene	54,000,000	
			Paleocene	65,000,000	
	Mesozoic		Cretaceous	136,000,000	Primates/Flowering Plants
			Jurassic	195,000,000	Birds
			Triassic	225,000,000	Dinosaurs/Mammals
	Paleozoic		Permian	320,000,000	Reptiles
			Pennsylvanian	345,000,000	Fern Forests
			Mississippian	395,000,000	Amphibians/Insects
			Devonian	430,000,000	Vascular Landplants
			Silurian	500,000,000	Fish/Chordates
Friday			Ordovician	570,000,000	Shellfish/Trilobites
			Cambrian	700,000,000	Multicellular Organisms
Thursday	Precambrian	Sunlight / Photosynthesis		1,400,000,000	Algae
Wednesday				2,100,000,000	Bacteriae
Tuesday		Amoebae /		2,800,000,000	Eucaryotic Cells
Monday		Endosymbiosis		3,500,000,000	Procaryotic Cells
Sunday		DNA/RNA		4,200,000,000	Mountains
Saturday	Formation of the Earth			4,900,000,000	Clay/Humic Acid

The timetable of evolution, left to right

In this picture you can see the Quranic Period on the left

1. **Then the Scientific era**
2. **Then the Scientific period**
3. **Then the epoch**
4. **Then the time in years**
5. **Then the type of organism**

The Quranic epoch in this metaphorical picture is approximately 700 million years long.

There was a bottleneck/extinction event 100,000 years ago, the Great Flood of Noah, pbuh, which happened Friday late afternoon of the Quranic period. Homo sapiens/Modern Man/Noah's People Homo Genus / came as a result of it, see book 6!

Human Beings are Adam's People and can be dated back to Homo erectus, around 1 million years ago.

<u>Quranic Periods in this picture compared to the scientific epochs, also explained in the Hadith:</u>

Quranic Friday afternoon:

Cenozoic - Grazing and carnivorous mammals

Quranic Friday Midday:

Mesozoic - Primates, flowering plants, birds and dinosaurs

Quranic Friday Morning:

Palaeozoic - Fish, reptiles, amphibians

Quranic Thursday:

Fern forests, insects vascular land plants, fish, chordates shellfish, and trilobites

Precambrian –

Quranic Wednesday:

Multicellular organisms, photosynthesis, sunlight, algae, bacteria, amoebae, eukaryotic cells

Quranic Tuesday: Endosymbiosis, procaryotic cells

Quranic Monday: DNA/RNA (tree of life, shjar-ul-khulud)

Quranic Sunday: Mountains

Quranic Saturday: Clay

Allah says about the different stages of the Earth's age:

"...Is it that ye deny Him Who created the Earth in 2 Days? ...

...He measured therein all things to give them nourishment in due proportion in 4 Days...

...He completed them as 7 heavens (layers) in 2 Days and He assigned to each heaven its duty and command..."

Surah Ha-Mim, 41 Ayah 9-12

This is the biological timekeeping which is explained on the previous 2 pages (1 youm is 700 million years of biological timekeeping). The next page explains the astronomical timekeeping!

The age of the Earth and the Universe

In the Quran the age of the Earth is two days (periods, youm) and the age of the Universe is 6 days. If we add another day for the last day, we have seven days. This is exactly a week. Scientists say that the age of the universe is 14-15 Billion years (see book 1).

Scientists say the Earth's age is 4-5 Billion years. This means the relation between the age of the Universe and the age of the Earth is 14: 4 or 7:2, just like in Surah Qaf, 50 Ayah 38. One day in the week of the Quran is 2 billion years in astronomical timekeeping. Allah has told us about the relation between the age of the Earth and the age of the Universe over 1400 years ago in the Quran.

(In this book the biological timekeeping is explained in detail, and there the length of the period or youm is 700 million years!)

The Prophet of Allah Mohammed (peace be upon him) said:

"Allah, the Exalted and Glorious, created the clay on Saturday and He created the mountains on Sunday and He created life on Monday and He created the things entailing labour (mukruh/loathsome) on Tuesday and created light on Wednesday and He caused the animals to spread on Thursday and created Adam (peace be upon him) after Asr on Friday, the last creation at the last hour of the hours of Friday, i.e. between afternoon and night"

Sahih Muslim Book 039 Hadith 6707, narrated by Abu Hurayrah

Reference Sahih Muslim 2789

(This Hadith explains the biological timekeeping in detail where each Quranic Period or youm is 700 million years as described on previous pages! In the astronomical timekeeping the Quranic Period or yuom is 2 billion years as described on previous pages.

Geochronological scale

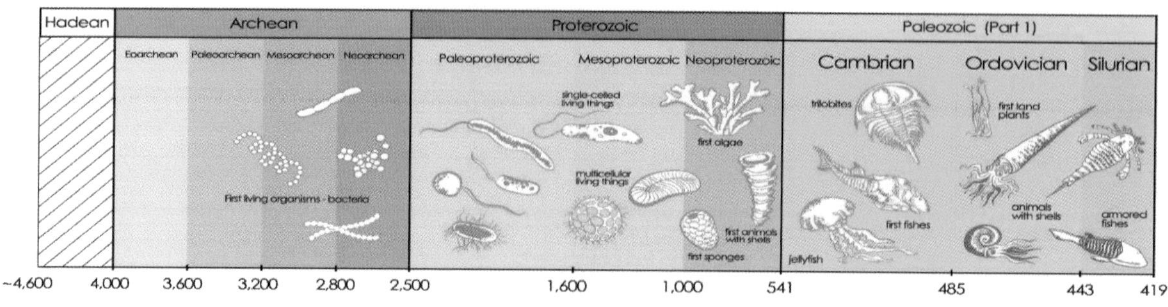

millions of years ago

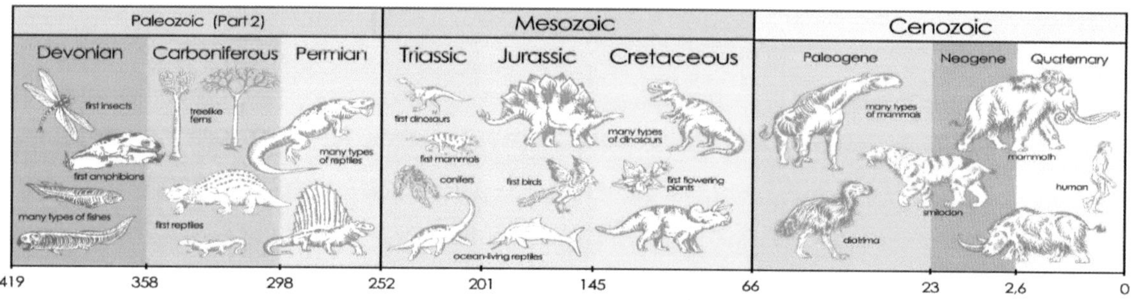

millions of years ago

This Hadith (story) shows how life on the Earth developed Life was there before light. Scientists thought until the 1970s that all life depends on the light of the sun. But they found out that at the bottom of the ocean there are chemo bacteria (extremophiles) living near hot black smokers from sulphur. They need no light. How could Mohammed (peace be upon him) have known this without being a Prophet? These bacteria are the oldest cells and they lived before sunlight could reach the surface of the Earth because of volcanic ash in the air. Plants developed after these chemo-or archaeobacteriae. Animals spread much later like the Hadith says. The things entailing labor are the mitochondriae or chloroplasts which developed out of chemo bacteria and are responsible for breathing inside animal cells and photosynthesis in all plant cells. The life/tree in this Hadith is the tree of life (shajar-ul-khulud) or the original cell/DNA. A weekday in this Hadith is around 700 Million (biolological timekeeping of the Quranic Period) or 0.7 Billion years (see page 14). This is the precise timetable of evolution=creation!

Allah also asks in the Quran:

"Say: "Is there any of your associates (who you think is equal to God], who produces creation then reproduces it?' Say: "Allah produces creation and reproduces it. How then are you mislead?"

Surah Yunus, 10 Ayah 34

"Those on whom ye call beside Allah will never create a fly though they combine together for the purpose."

Surah Al-Hajj, 22 Ayah 73

Can we create life?

With these verses Allah explains that only he can create creatures again and again. Also, after our death he will recreate us all, animals and humans.

He also tells us that no one else can do this. Even genetics allows us only to copy Allah's creation. So, we are not playing God and creating new life, like many atheists like to say, but merely using the code of life which Allah has given, the genetic code, the genes.

Some scientists misuse genes and others use it for good purposes such as healing sick people.

In any case, the decree of life is contained in this universe, which is a creation of Allah. Even the cosmic dust or stardust contains the ability to evolve into live, as it has been given this property, characteristic, ability, quality, or feature by its Creator.

So even if we are using atoms or subatomic particles, we are just using the tools that Allah has given, and not actually creating anything!

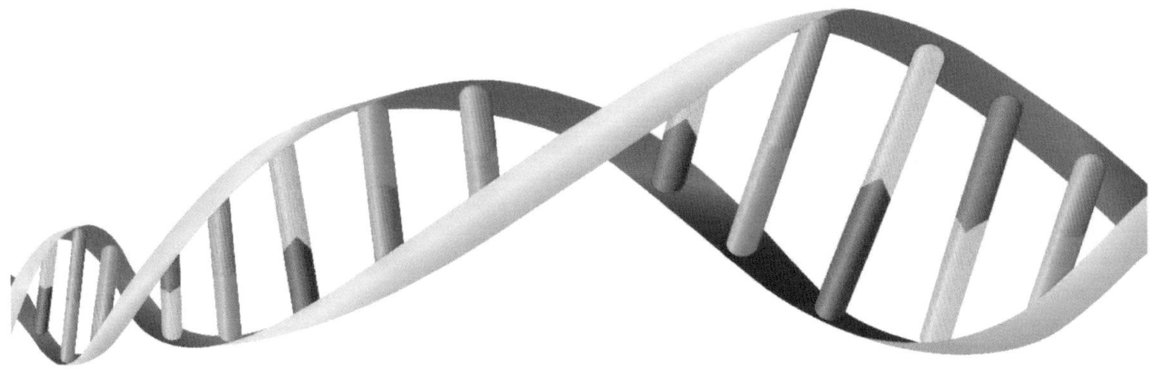

Summary 1

In the Quran Allah has revealed exact details about evolution, which is just another word for creation. Most religious people do not believe in evolution, although it is described in the Quran. Many scientists do not believe in Allah because they think Islam is against evolution. That is not true at all. The Quran says that Allah is the one who made evolution happen. Many scientists think that animals changed without any purpose other than survival. In the Quran there are also exact details about how old the Earth is and how old the whole universe is.

There is also a Hadith (story) about the exact way evolution of life on our planet Earth has happened...

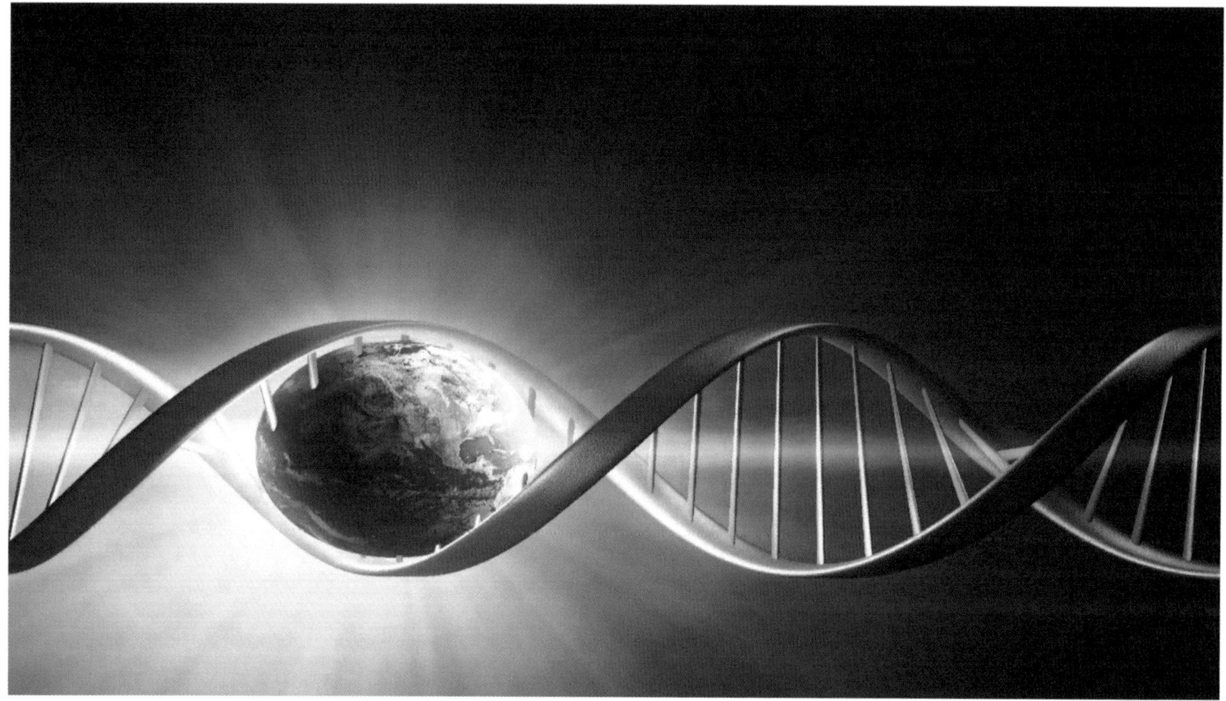

Summary 2

These are scientific discoveries of the 20th century and have been proven to be true by using new machines less than 20-30 years ago.

The Quran was revealed to the Prophet Mohammed (peace be upon him) 1400 years ago at a time when submarines, satellites or microscopes did not exist.

The Quran is a revelation of Allah, the Creator. These are only a few of Allah's signs. There are many more.

There is no God but Allah
And Mohammed is The Messenger of Allah

Part 6
Biology
Humans

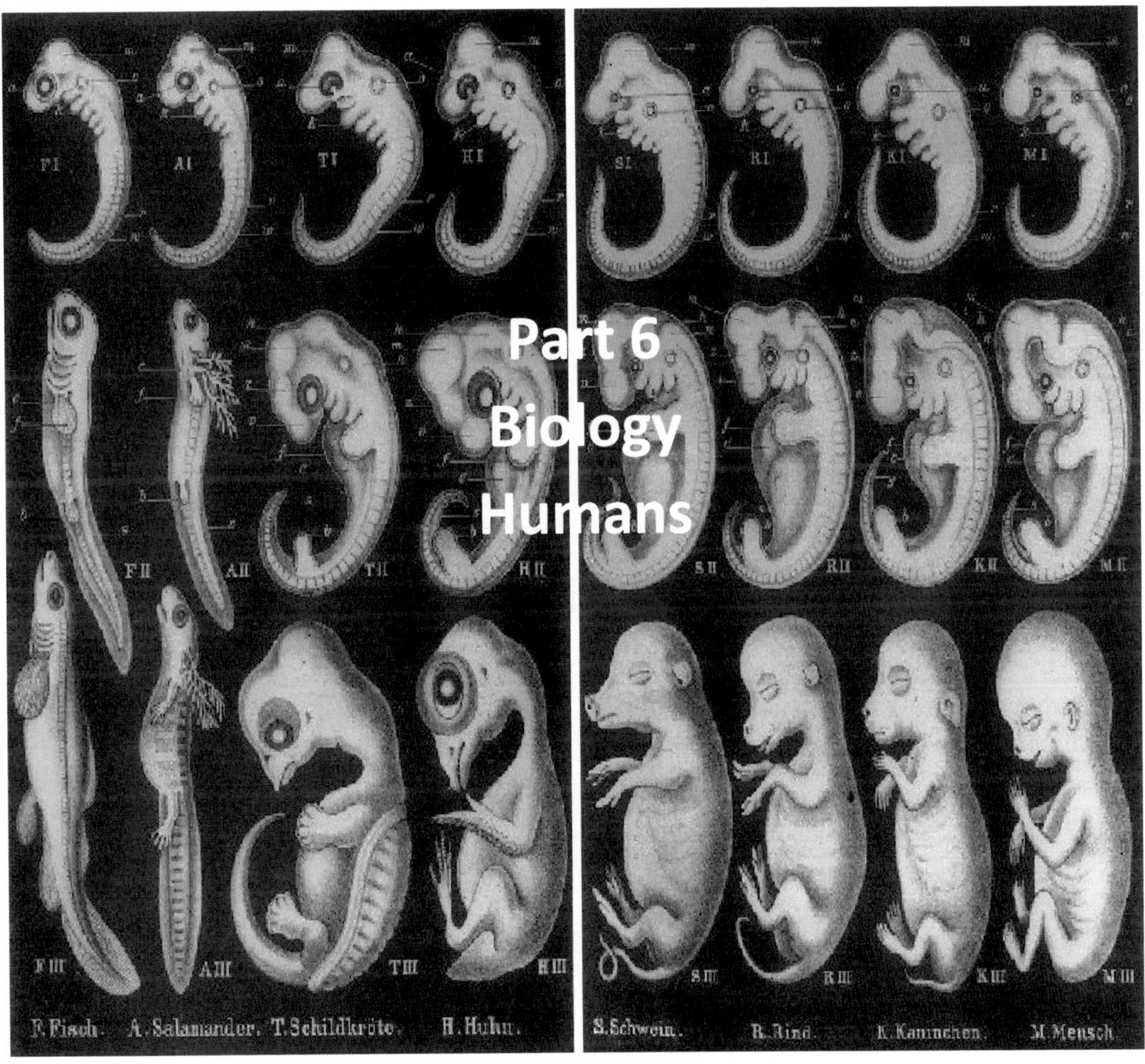

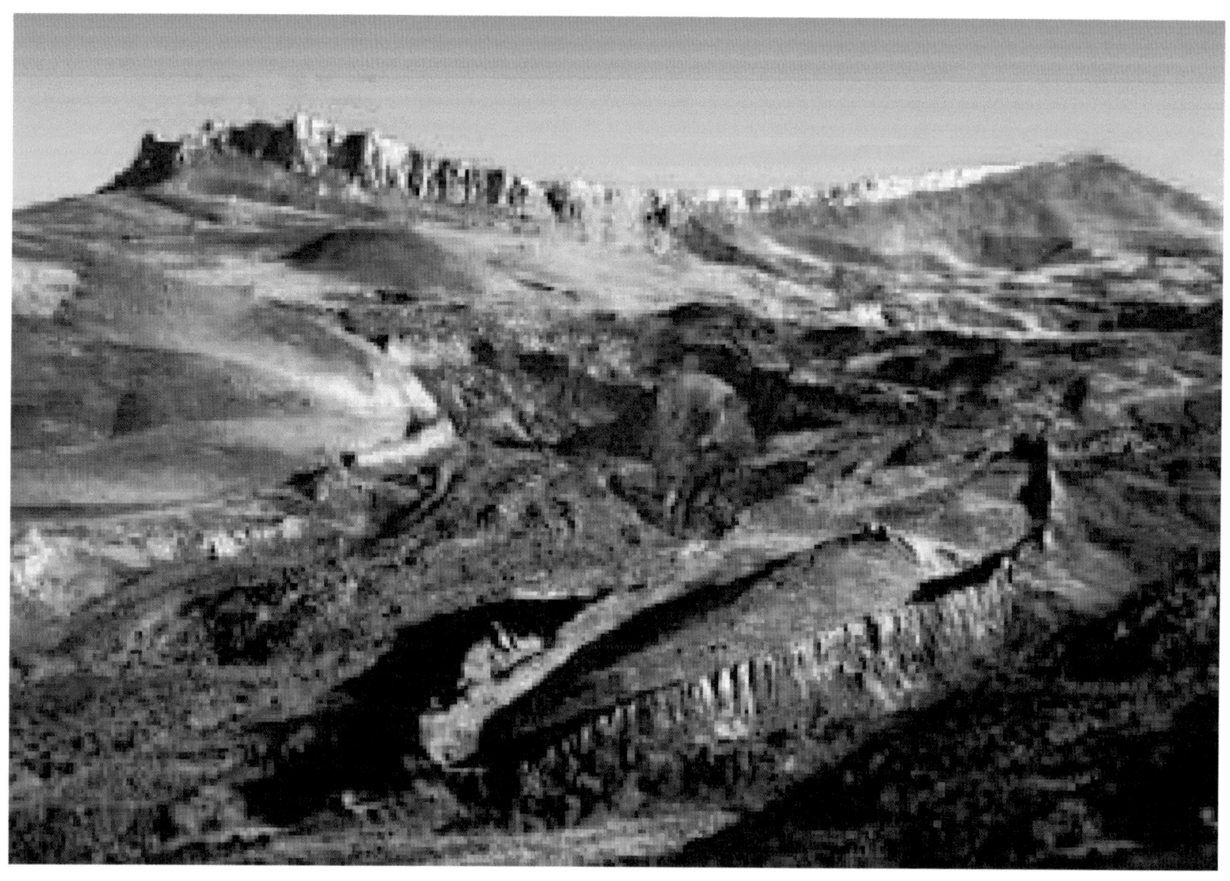

In the name of Allah, The Most Forgiving, Most Merciful.

In the Quran Allah commands us to...

"... Travel through the Earth and see how Allah made creation happen..."
Surah Al-Ankabut, 29 Ayah 20

This is a command of Allah, and we must take his command seriously. Most religious people don't really follow Allah's command, although Allah says about mankind:

"Indeed, I created mankind as the best of organisms"
Surah Al-Tin, 95 Ayah 4

Allah also said 1400 years ago:

"If Allah wanted, He could destroy you and appoint in your place people whom He wants as successors just as He brought you forth from the descendants of other peoples."

Surah Al-Anam, 6 Ayah 133

Allah could destroy and replace us anytime if he wanted. He also points out that we descend from other peoples. So there have been many different species of mankind before. Scientists call these Hominoids, like Homo erectus, Homo habilis and Homo sapiens, our species. All Hominoids are one genus (family).

Allah created us from clay:

"...Indeed We created them of sticky clay."

Surah Al-Saffat, 37 Ayah 11

"...We began the creation of humankind from clay"

Surah Al Sajdah, 32 Ayah 7

"...We created humankind from clay ..."

Surah Al Hijr, 15 Ayah 26

Clay has all the necessary substances for life, mainly Carbon and many minerals. We all are carbon-based life forms and so are animals and plants. Nitrogen, Oxygen and Hydrogen which Allah also used in the creation of life, are abundant in the air and water on planet Earth (see Surah Al-Anbiyaa, 21 Ayah 30 and Surah AlFurqan, 25 Ayah 54).

Of course, all these substances are Allah's creations as well.

Allah turned people in the past into apes and pigs as a punishment for their sins:

"... We said to them: "Be ye apes despised and rejected."

Surah Al-Baqara, 2 Ayah 65

"...He transformed into apes and swines those who worshipped Evil"

Surah Al-Maida, 5 Ayah 60

"Be ye apes despised and rejected."

Surah Al-A'raf, 7 Ayah 166

97-99% of the genes of apes are the same as ours. Around 95% of the genes of pigs are the same as ours also. Both are in many ways exactly like humans. Apes are similar in behaviour and pigs in terms of their inner organs and anatomy. Pigs, apes and humans are omnivores.

Apes and pigs are similar to us in many ways:

Apes' brains are like ours and they can do many of the things we can. Pigs' organs are very close to humans and pigs' hearts can even be transplanted into our bodies to replace our hearts.

Eating meat from pigs and apes is forbidden because it is like cannibalism (eating one's own species) and unhealthy. There are all sorts of diseases in it. Ape meat contains HIV and can cause AIDS. Pig meat has many hormones and a lot of urea so it causes tooth decay, stress and accelerates the aging process. There are many more reasons for not eating these meats, like toxins, viruses, and parasites.

Pigs are meant for the woodland and not the farm. Inside a closed stable they sit in their own dirt and become very dirty. This does not happen in the wild. Their meat is unclean. They have important roles in the ecosystem, like digging roots and the earth to soften it and remove poison from the earth. We have to protect them, and they belong into the forests and not on farms or on our plates as dinner! Neither should we eat ape-meat!

There are also new theories in science which we still need to explore. Many of them will be covered by the Quran.

There is a new theory in biology that says that apes descend from early Hominoids or their forefathers, Australopithecines, who walked upright like us. This theory would confirm that part of the early Hominoids or Australopithecines kept walking upright and were turned into modern humans and others went back to trees and were turned into Apes. Allah said that 1400 years ago. But this is not proven yet, so we must study science and explore it. There is also a missing fossil-link between monkeys and Australopithecines, and some say there is a missing link between apes and Hominoids. But still, they think we descend from apes and animals. But in fact, apes descend from humans and humans are a separate creation as Allah says:

"...then We developed out of it another creature...!"
Surah Al-Muminoon, 23 Ayah 14

There is a Hadith speaking about these apes dying without having any children. The above verses are repeated in the Quran, so this is a habit of Allah. Maybe other ancient apes might have survived.

We all descend from Noah's family and companions who were carried on the Ark during the big flood. Noah's family descended from Adam's family:

“We saved him and the Companions of the Ark and We made the (Ark) a Sign for all Peoples!"

Surah Al-Ankabut, 29 Ayah 15

"We when the water (of Noah's flood) overflowed beyond its limits carried you (mankind) in the floating (Ark)."

Surah Al-Haqqa, 69 Ayah 11

"O ye that are sprung from those whom We carried (in the Ark) with Noah..."

Surah Al-Israa, 17 Ayahs 3

Therefore, it could be said that modern man (Homo Sapiens) is Noah's tribe, and the early humans or Hominoids were Adam's tribe.

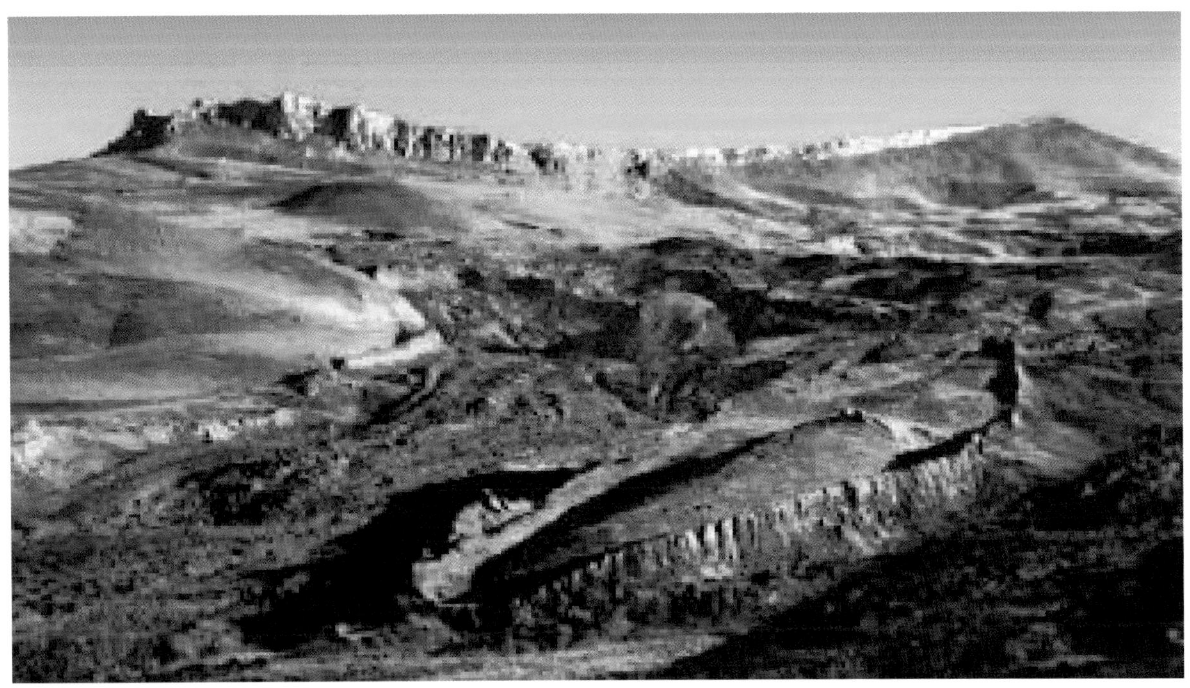

This is the fossilized Ark found on Mount Judi as seen from a satellite.

It has been estimated that the fossilised remains of the Ark and modern man (Homo Sapiens) are of the same age!

Biologists know that there has been a so-called bottleneck before Homo sapiens, the modern humans came about. This means that there were very few Hominoids left from whom we all descend. All others were killed. It is also true that Hominoids migrated across continents very early (over 1 Million years ago).

The oldest fossilized Homo sapiens skull is around 150000 years old. This is the same age as the fossilized ark which is shown above. The Ark remains were found in Mount Judi like Allah says in the Koran and not in Mount Ararat like the Bible says, see next page. The Ark found was big enough to carry all species of animals.

So, all present humans descend from the small group of humans around Noah that lived around 150000 years ago. This can also be proven with latest genetic methods (mitochondrial DNA). We need to find out, if this genetic proof is also possible in animals to establish the flood scientifically:'(It seems to be the case in many mammals).

Finally, as in Sahih Muslim Hadith 6707, narrated by Abu Hurairah which is in book 5 of this series, man (Adam) was created by Allah only very recently, shortly before the end. This confirms the fact, that the Homo genus (family, see page 4) has only appeared around 1 Million years ago, whereas planet Earth is 4, 5 Billion years old.

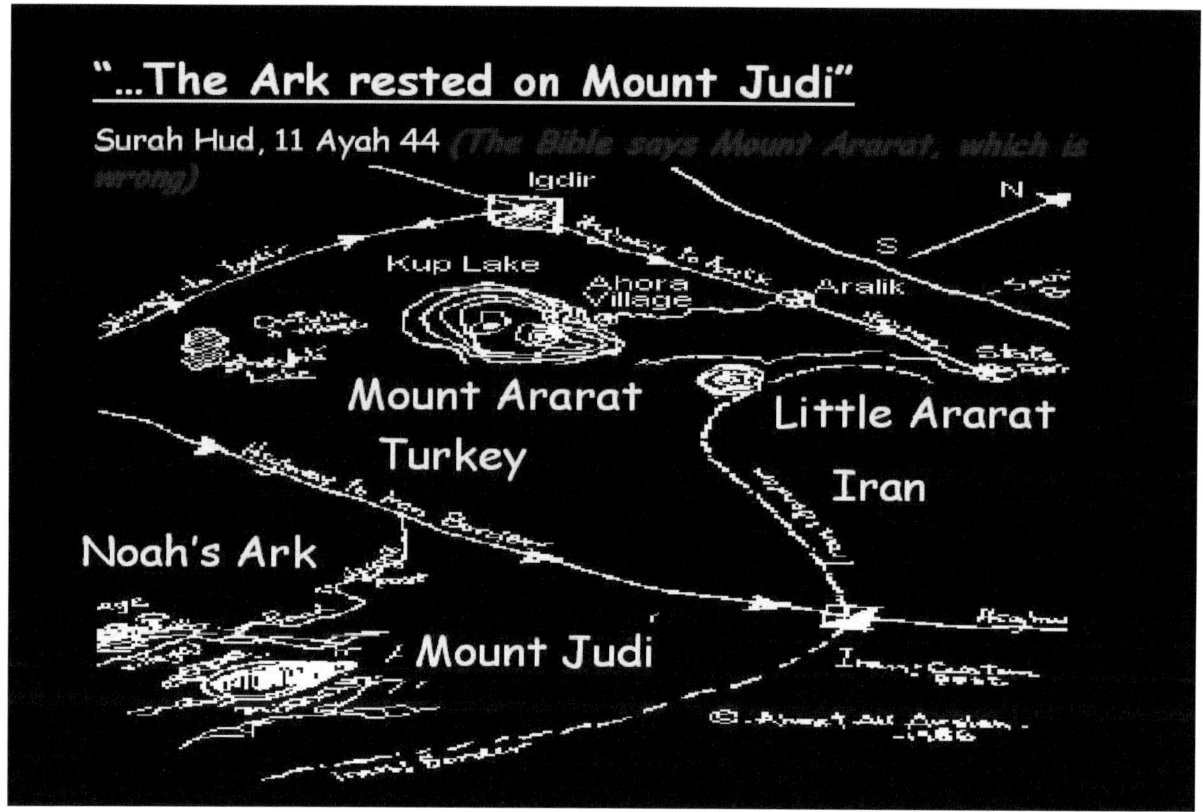

"A Sign for them is that we created their race (through the flood) in the loaded Ark;"

Surah Ya-Sin Surah 36 Ayah 41

Allah created us in different stages inside the wombs of our mothers. The bones develop as a cartilage first and are then surrounded by muscles. Only after that the bones become hard:

"Man, We did create from a quintessence (of clay); Then We placed him as (a drop of) sperm in a place of rest firmly fixed; Then We made the sperm into a clot of congealed blood; then of that clot We made a (foetus) lump; then We made out of that lump bones and clothed the bones with flesh..."

Surah Al-Muminun, 23 Ayahs 12-14

"Created man out of a (mere) clot of blood"

Surah Al-Alaq, 96 Ayah 2

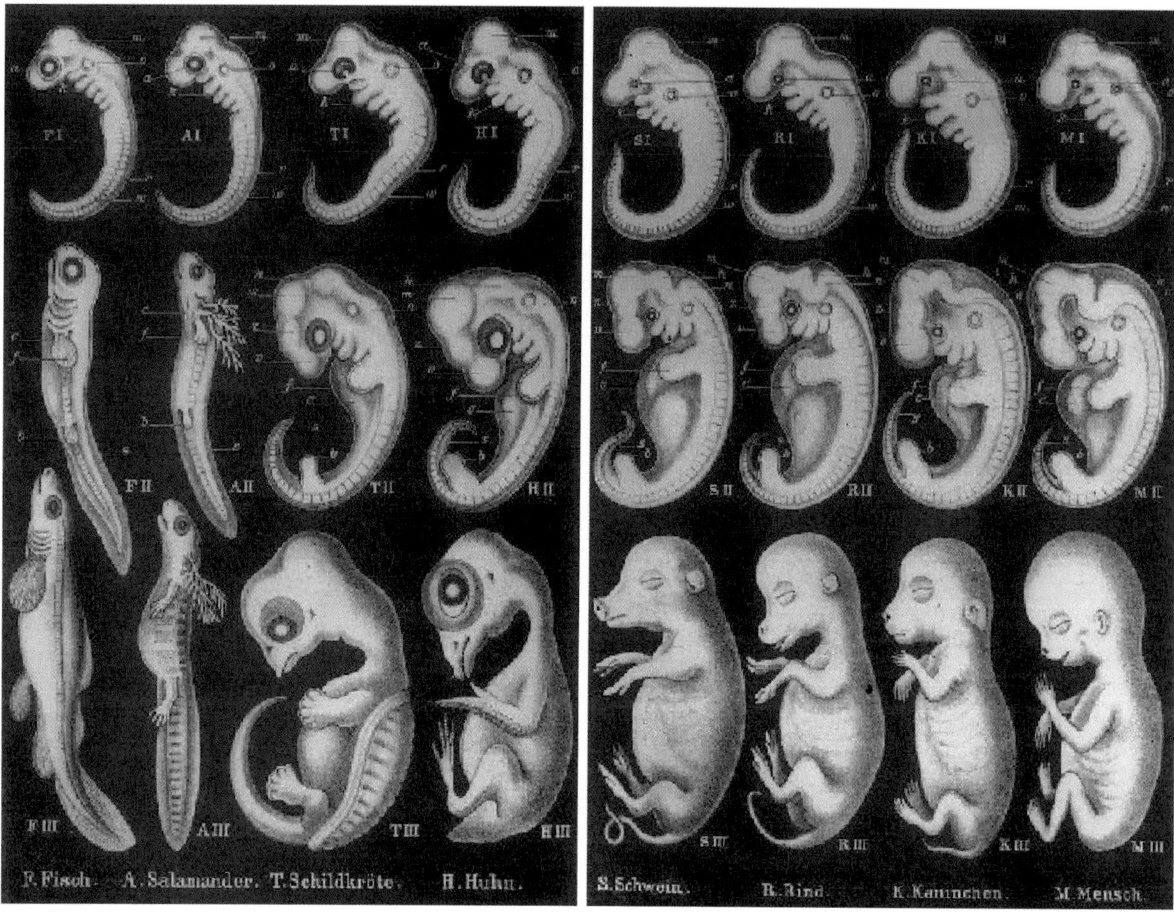

Vertebrate embryos look very similar in the early stages of development. At the end all of a sudden, the human embryo is metamorphosed into a completely different being (See Surah Al-Muminun, 23 Ayah 12-14).

This picture shows the embryos of:

Shark, Amphibian, Lizard, Chicken, Pig, Rodent, Monkey, Man

<u>Allah used earth, clay, and water to create us:</u>

"...Seeing that it is He that has created you in diverse stages? ...And Allah has produced you from the earth growing ..."

Surah Nuh, 71 Ayahs 14-18

"...He created man from sounding clay like pottery"

Surah Ar-Rahman, 55 Ayah 14

"...It is He Who has created man from water...!

Surah Al-Furqaan, 25 Ayah 54

Science confirms that earth and clay contain all the necessary ingredients for life and that clay supports the embryological growth. Many women crave for it during pregnancy. Science also confirms that life comes from earth.

"Then We made him a sperm-drop in a firm resting place.

Then We turned the sperm-drop into a clot, then We turned the clot into a fetus-lump, then We turned the fetus-lump into bones, then We clothed the bones with flesh; thereafter We developed it <u>into another creature</u>. So, glorious is Allah, the Best of the Creators."

Surah Al-Muminun, 23 Ayah 13&14

This is exactly how the foetus develops. There are detailed books about it which you should study if you are interested. The important part is highlighted in red above, after a similar development in the womb like animals, <u>Allah turns us into another creature!</u>

"Does human think that We will never assemble his bones? Yes, indeed, We are able to make whole his very fingertips."
Surah Al Qiyama, 75 Ayah 3&4

This Verse refers to the uniqueness of the fingerprint and indicates that genetic fingerprinting is like it, long before both were discovered. It also points to the genetic relatedness of the fingerprints and the limb-bones which has recently been discovered.

"...He makes you in the wombs of your mothers in stages one after another in three veils of darkness."
Surah Az-Zumar, 39 Ayah 6

There are three cell-layers between the embryo and the environment as can be seen on the following page.

"Now let man but think from what he is created! He is created from a drop emitted Proceeding from between the backbone and the ribs (or from backbone into ribs)"
Surah At-Tariq, 86 Ayahs 5-7

We develop the backbone first, then the ribs. Many organs develop between these two as can be seen a few pages later. And this is also where the embryo grows inside the mother's body to become a fetus.

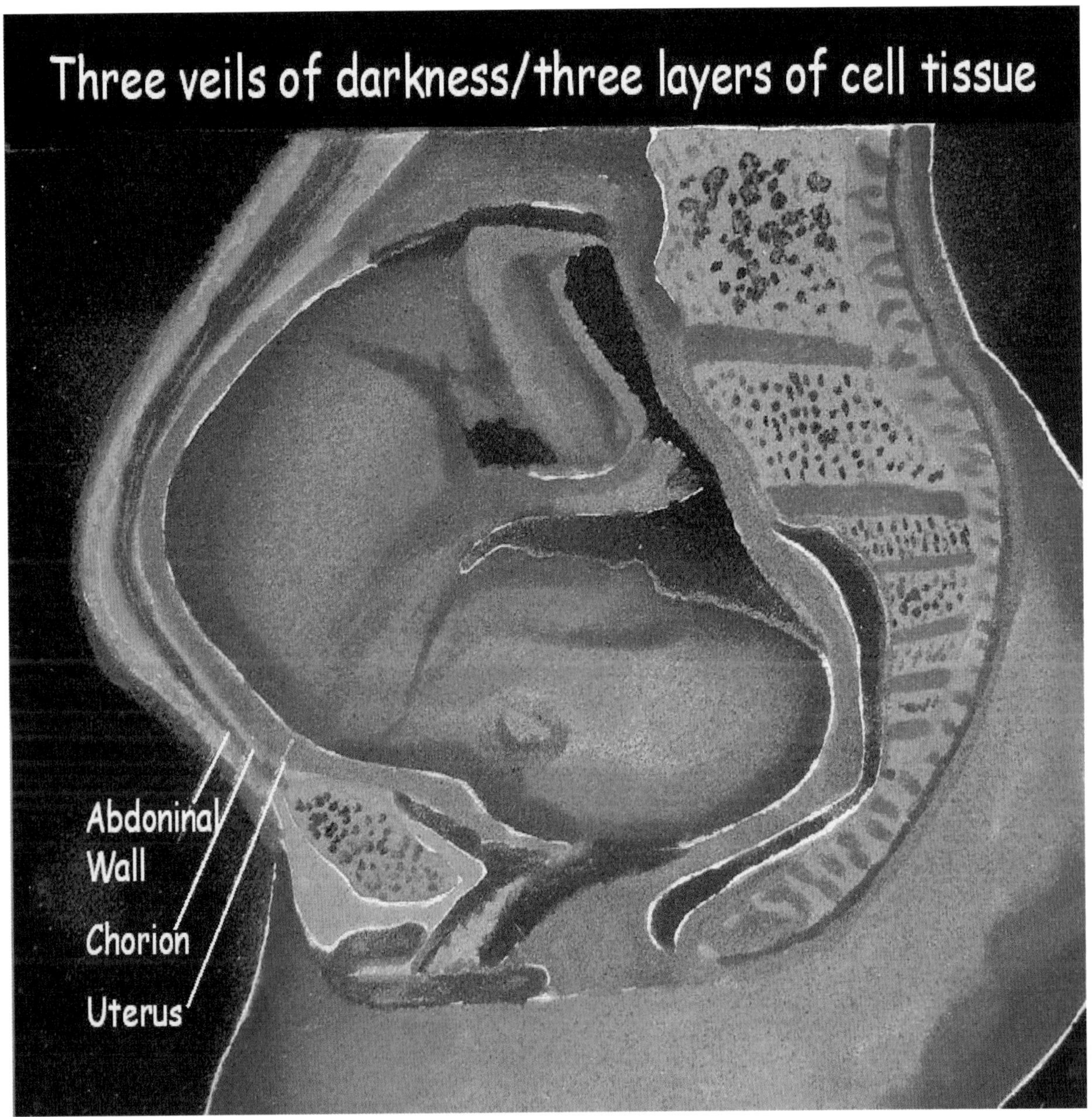

Three veils of darkness/three layers of cell tissue:

Abdominal Wall
Chorion
Uterus

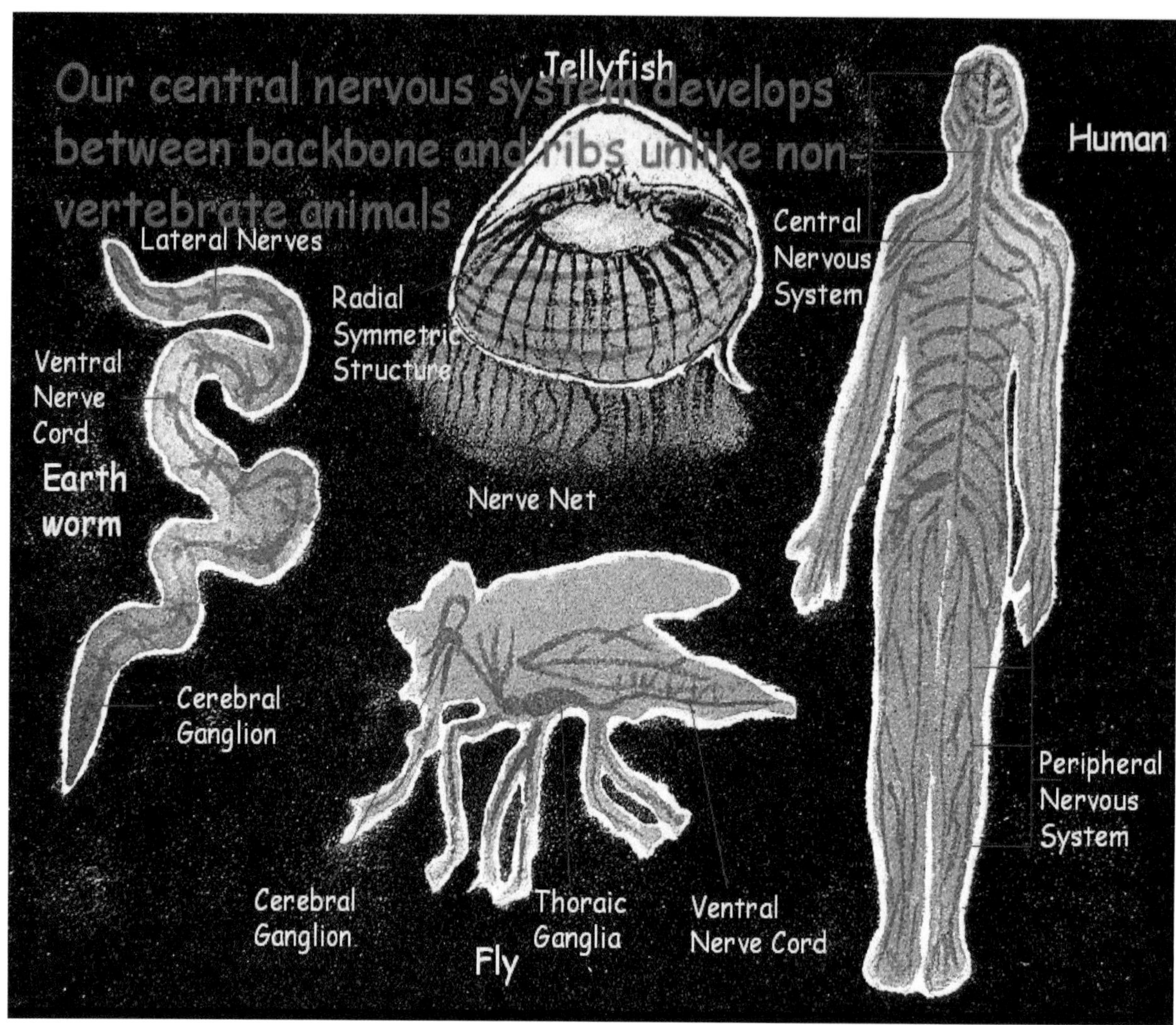

"Now let man but think from what he is created! He is created from a drop emitted Proceeding from between the backbone and the ribs (or from backbone into ribs)"

Surah At-Tariq, 86 Ayahs 5-7

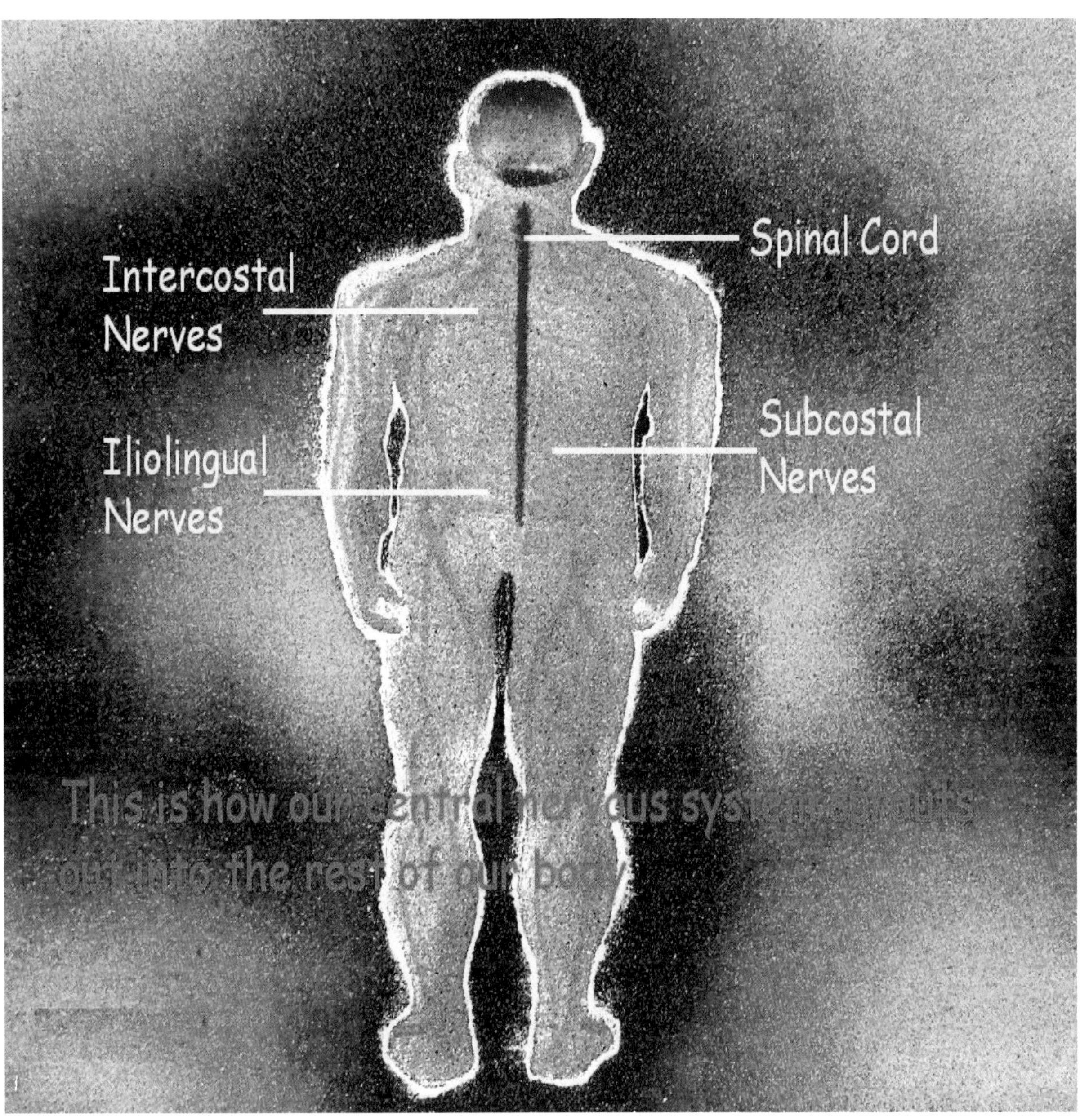

"Now let man but think from what he is created! He is created from a drop emitted Proceeding from between the backbone and the ribs (or from backbone into ribs)"

Surah At-Tariq, 86 Ayahs 5-7

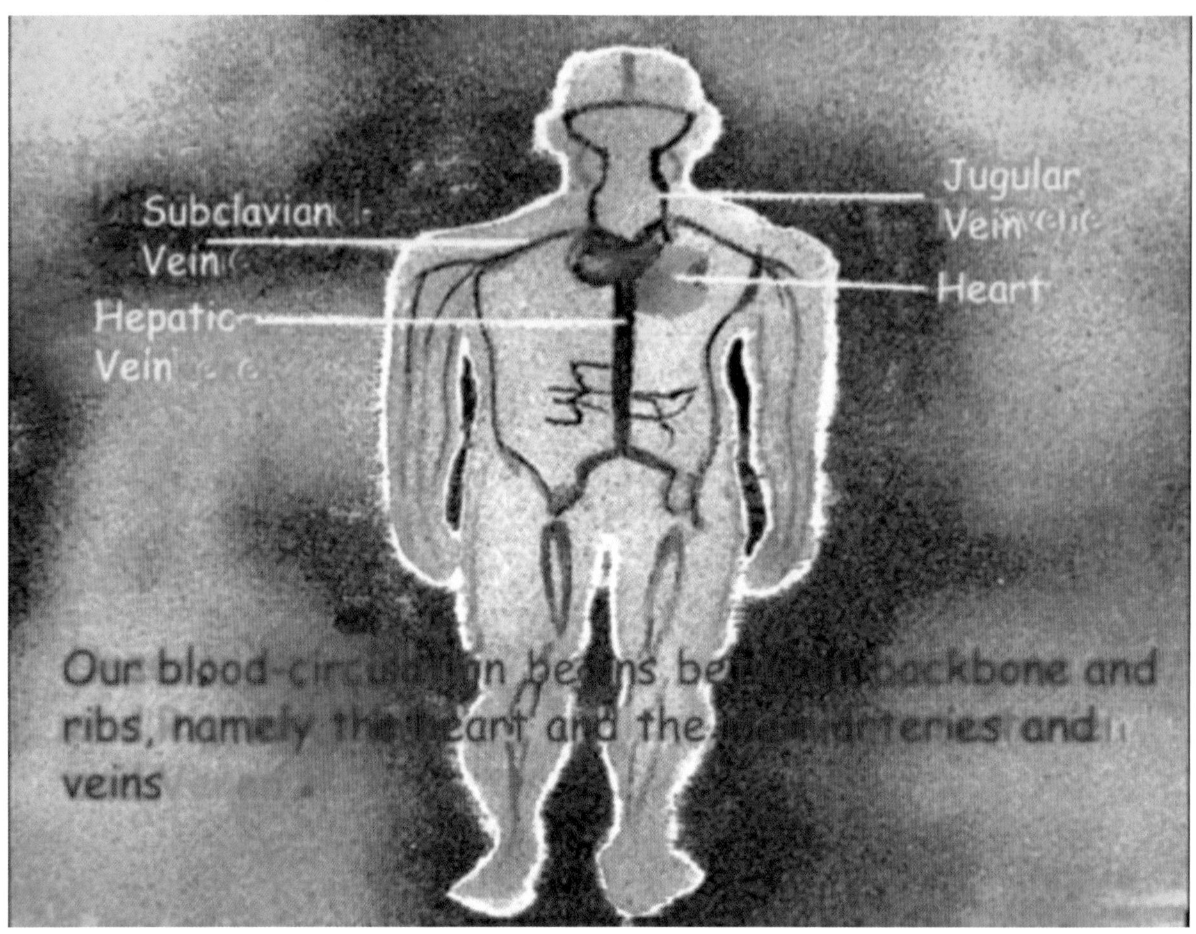

"Now let man but think from what he is created! He is created from a drop emitted Proceeding from between the backbone and the ribs (or from backbone into ribs)"

Surah At-Tariq, 86 Ayahs 5-7

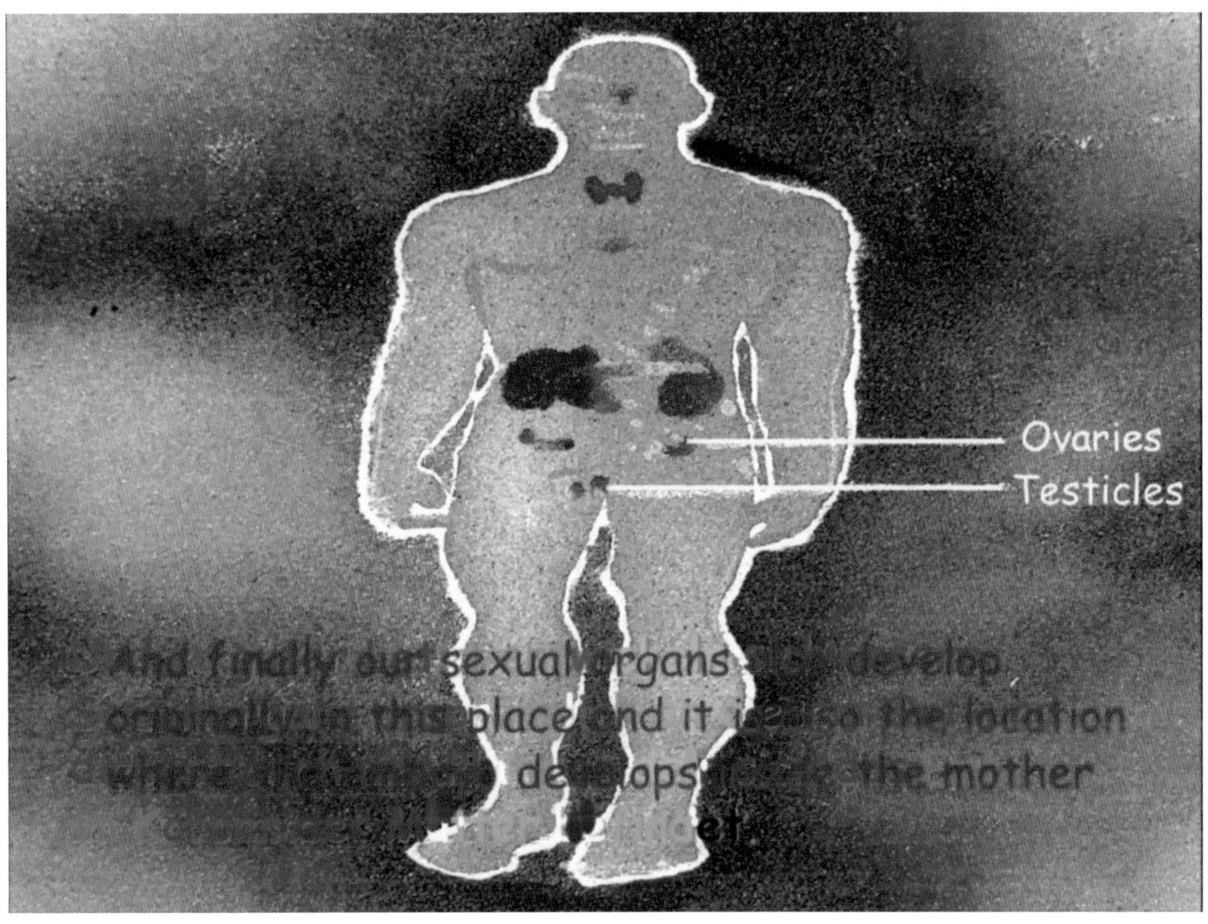

"Now let man but think from what he is created! He is created from a drop emitted Proceeding from between the backbone and the ribs (or from backbone into ribs)"

Surah At-Tariq, 86 Ayahs 5-7

"He determines the two genders from a drop of semen when it is emitted."

Surah An-Najm 53, Ayah 45-46

This is s fact that cannot be known without detailed modern genetic research and analysis. It was only discovered very recently that the gender of the child is determied through the semen, and that the sperm from the father (and not the ovum from the mother) carries either two x or an x and a y chromosome in the 23rd pair that is responsible for gender determination

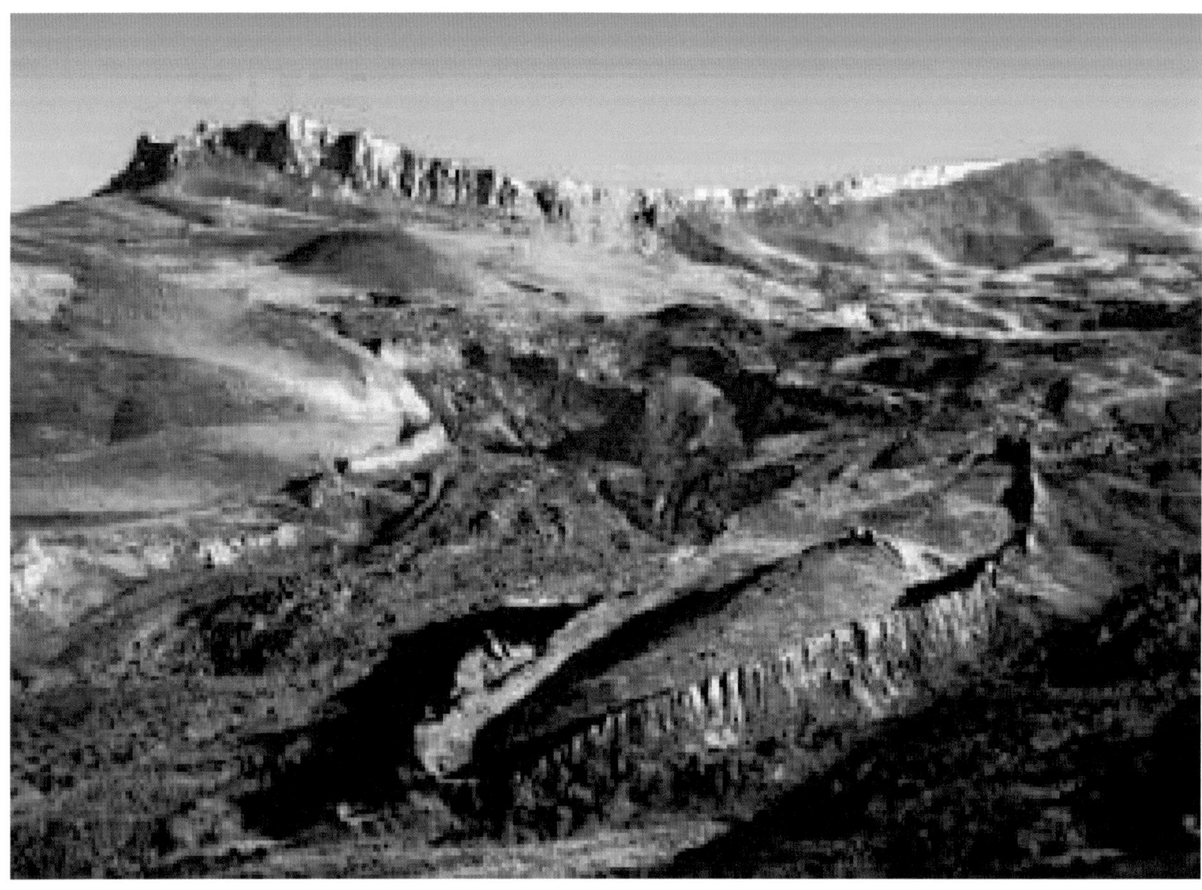

Summary

In the Koran Allah has revealed exact details about the way humans have descended from other people (Hominoids). He also describes therein that some pigs and apes descend from men and not the other way around. Most religious people do not believe in this although it is written in the Koran. But Hominoids were created separately from animals although their embryological development looks similar.

Allah also describes Noah's Ark that rested on Mount Judi after the flood, which is exactly where it was found in a fossilised form. It is furthermore just as old as modern man, Homo Sapiens, 100,000-200,000 years. Many scientists don't believe in religion because they think that all religions are against evolution, which isn't true. The Koran says that Allah is the One Who made evolution happen. Many scientists believe that man descends from apes and not the other way around like the Koran says, although there are indications for it. Many religious people don't know that either.

The Koran also gives exact descriptions on how we develop inside the wombs of our mothers and that there are three cell-layers between us and the environment when we are there. Our development from backbone towards ribs or in between both is also described in the Koran. Gender determination through the father's semen is explained in the Quran which was not known until 20-30 years ago.

The Koran is clearly a revelation from Allah, the Creator.

These are only a few of Allah's signs. There are many more...

There is no God but Allah
and Mohammed is The Messenger of Allah

Part 7
The 5 Pillars

In the name of Allah, the most Forgiving, the most Merciful

-

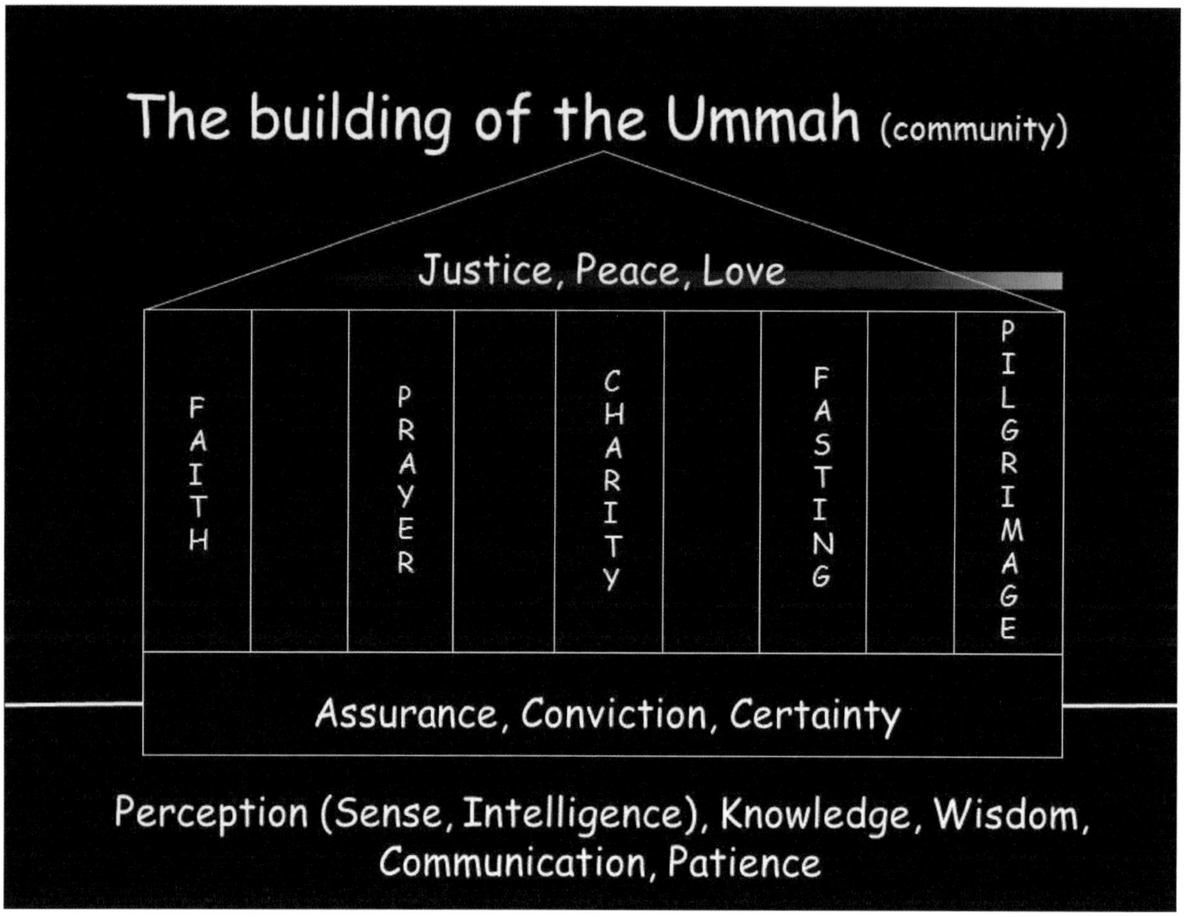

The building of the Ummah (community)

Justice, Peace, Love

FAITH

PRAYER

CHARITY

FASTING

PILGRIMAGE

Assurance, Conviction, Certainty

Perception (Sense, Intelligence), Knowledge, Wisdom, Communication, Patience

Ummah (community building)

Roof
Justice, Peace, Love
Pillar
Faith, Prayer, Charity (Zakat), Fasting (Roza), Pilgrimage (Hajj)
Foundation
Assurance, Confidence, Certainty
Soil
Perception (feeling, intelligence,) Knowledge, Wisdom, Communication, Patience (Patience)

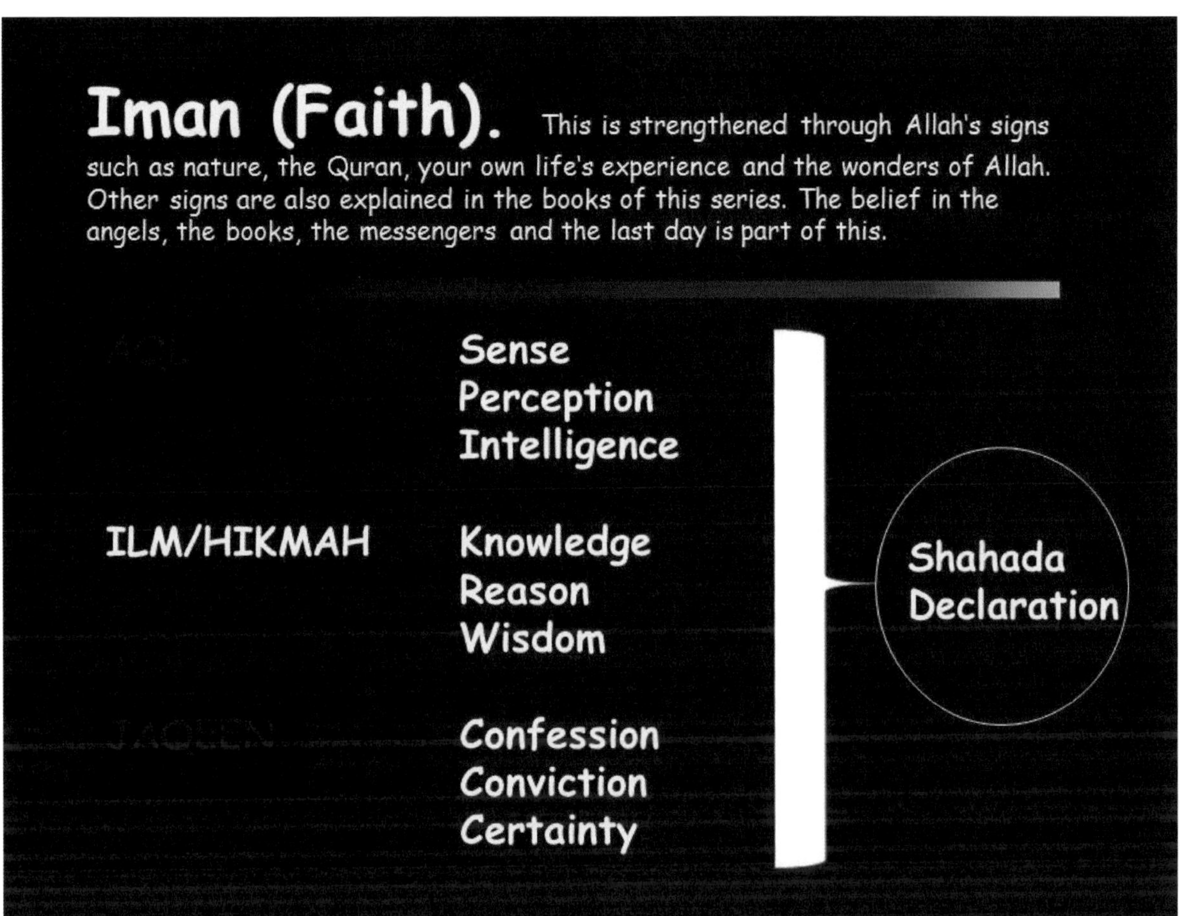

Iman (Faith).

This is strengthened through Allah's signs such as nature, the Quran, your own life's experience and the wonders of Allah. Other signs are also explained in the books of this series. The belief in the angels, the books, the messengers and the last day is part of this.

Sense Perception Intelligence AQAL-

Knowledge Reason Wisdom ILM/HIKMAH-

Confession Conviction Certainty YAQEEN-

Shahada Declaration Leads to the-

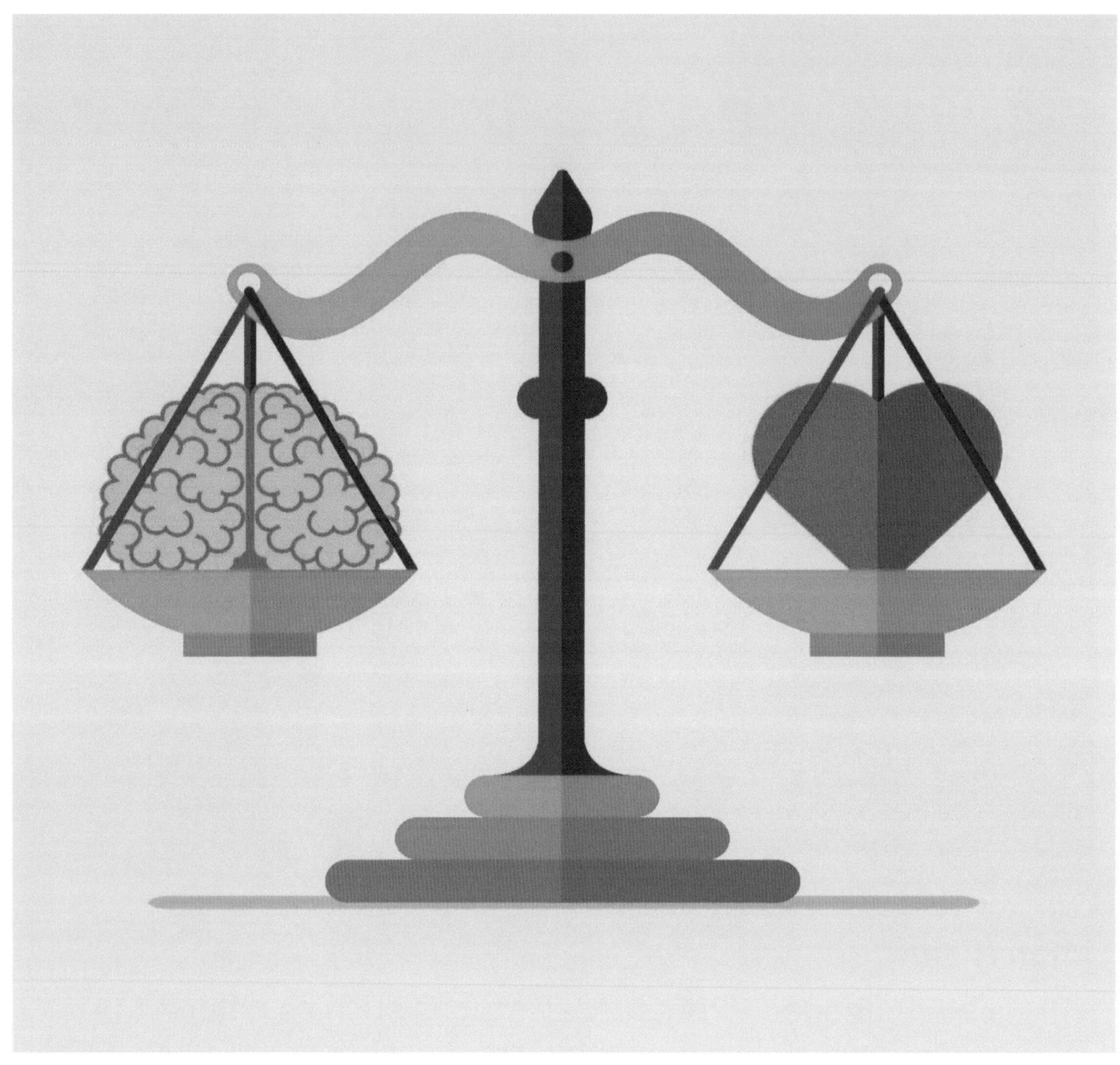

Iman (Faith) with Reason!

Real faith is based on reason and sense, not on fanaticism or stubbornness. The original faith of our Prophet Mohammed, peace be upon him (pbuh) wasn't blind! It was one of true conviction and certainty.

The Faith is declared by the statement (Shahada), "La ilaha illal llah, Mohammadur Rasoul Ullllah." This means, no deity apart from Allah, Mohammed is the Messenger of Allah. That is the manifestation of the Islamic faith, the absolute truth and the fabric of the universe. From this, all teachings of Islam are derived as well as all rituals and habits.

The Faith in Islam consists of believing in Allah, His Books, His Angels, His Messengers, and the Last Day of Judgement. It also includes believing in Paradise and Hell and in Satan, an evil Jinn or spirit Allah has created to test us.

At school and in universities today we are taught that the faith in God isn't compatible with reason and progress. But most scientists say that the existence of God cannot be proved or disapproved by science. In reality though His existence is clearly proven by the many verses listed and explained in the first 6 books of this series. Allah is the Creator of all things and beings. This understanding of faith is not very widely known or accepted unfortunately, and many religious people as well as scientists today still believe that all religions are contradictory to science and technology. In reality they are mainly referring to Christianity and the Church.

In fact, most scientists haven't even engaged properly with the Quran and most Muslims haven't engaged with sciences, otherwise they would know that the Quran is clearly compatible with the scientific discoveries of the last 50 years and all current knowledge about nature. The scientific signs listed in books 1-6 are some of the many proofs for our faith and arguments for debate in this century. There are many more.

Salah (Service Prayer)

The Prayer is done 5 times daily, in the morning, midday, in the afternoon, in the evening and at night before bedtime. It is for worshipping Allah only. The Kaaba as the central direction serves as a symbol of unity of all Muslims.

Origins

This act of worship or prayer, in its present form, was given to our Prophet Muhammad (peace be upon him) during the Ascension, even above the seventh heaven. Even before the Prophet Muhammad (peace be upon him) people performed such acts of worship and supplications as we can see today in its early form in all nations, e.g. They also kneel, bow and prostrate, as can be seen in the case of priests, monks, etc. This practice also confirms the fact that worship was practiced in their religions as well. That is why this pure form of worship and supplication, in its modern form, was revealed to our Prophet Muhammad (peace be upon him) again. Even Adam, Abraham, Moses, David, Solomon, and Jesus all prayed and worshiped God in the same way, as can be seen in the Bible.

The service-or ritual-prayer was only revealed 10 years after the first line of the Quran to our Prophet Mohammed, pbuh, towards the end of his time in Mecca, when his companions were asking him for a better form of communication with Allah. So, they were motivated and strong in faith, which is a pre-condition for prayer. Every Muslim is supposed to conduct it from the age of 11 onward. Shortly after the ordainment of the prayer the Muslims had to leave Mecca, because it angered the unbelievers too much and they saw it as a threat to their lifestyle. They started torturing and persecuting the Muslims and wanted to kill our Prophet Mohammed, pbuh. Of course, prayer can save a person from hellfire. It is not meant for those who are aiming for it, because even one sincere prostration can save you from it.

From the scientific perspective, prayer and meditation are the best relief for stress! Stress is the biggest killer today and cause for sickness and problems in society. Prayer distracts from stress and problems, remembrance of Allah eradicates the stress, mentioning Allah takes away depression through repentance you become happy! Allah also solves your problems and finds the best solutions for you, you will see it for yourself, how you will become happy and successful and pass the small obstacles easily!

Wudu´

Salah (Service Prayer)

The service prayer is conducted in the direction of Mecca (the Qibla) and nobody should pass immediately in front of the person praying. The Kaaba (house) in Mecca was built by Abraham and Ismael (peace be upon them) around 3000 years ago.

Wudhu (Ritual - Washing)

The cleanliness of the body and teeth is very important in Islam. Particularly, the washing after toilet and intercourse. In this way, fungi, haemorrhoids and unfriendly bacteria are kept at bay. By using water, Allah's throne, one gets closer to Him.

The ritual-washing begins with the hands, then the mouth, the nose, the face, the lower arms to the elbows, the head, the ears, the neck, the feet, always right first then left, symmetrically approaching the heart. One uses cold or luke-warm water. In winter, one can also use warm water. This process is also used in modern rheuma-therapy. After travel, intercourse, or menstruation one has to wash the whole body in a particular way, called Ghusl.

The ritual-washing invigorates the nerves and the blood-circulation, purifies the skin and soft-tissues and in winter one should use creme or oil afterwards to avoid dry skin. That should be rubbed into the moist skin saying Bismillah, in Allah's Glory. While travelling and if there is a lack of water, one is allowed to simply rub sand or soil into the hands and forehead. That is called Tayyamum.

In this way one stays clean, healthy, the blood-circulation is supported, and one smells good. The washing of the soft-tissue protects from infections such as the flu, environmental pollution such as ash-particles, dust and free radicals and works as a prevention of cancer. The water should be running and not stale. It should be from a fresh stream, ideally.

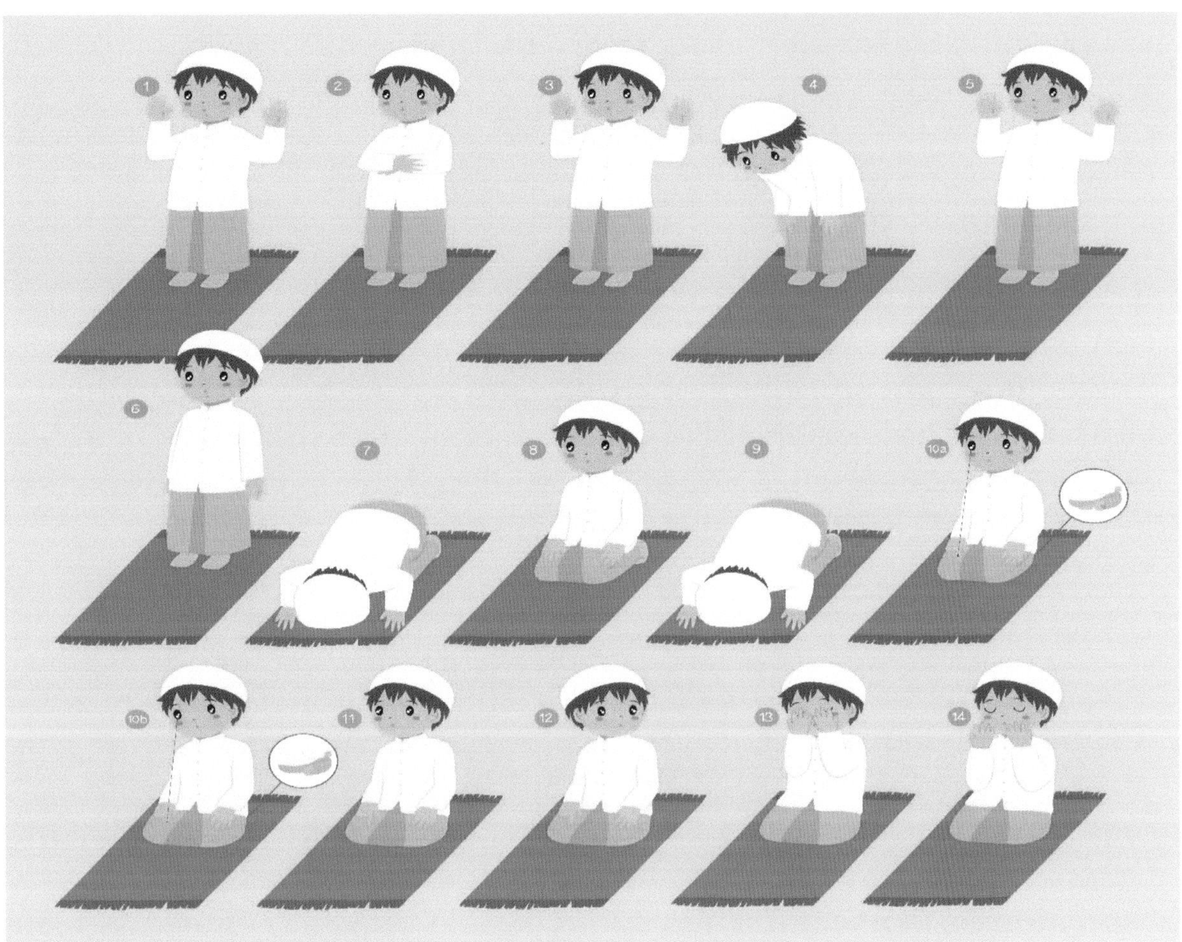

Salah (Service Prayer)

One period (Rakah) has 5 consecutive positions, standing, bowing, prostrating, kneeling, prostrating, kneeling and then back to standing. The Kaaba in Mecca has been the only direction since the time of Mohammed, pbuh, and the destination for the pilgrimage.

Times

First there were supposed to be 50 prayers, but Moses, pbuh, whom Mohammed, pbuh, met on the way to the 7th heaven, asked him to to go back repeatedly during the Meraj and ask for a reduction of the number. The special significance of this is Allah's Mercy through our Prophet Mohammed, pbuh, with support from Moses, pbuh. Since then, all good deeds count 10-fold. So, in effect the 5 prayers are worth 50 prayers as well as all other good deeds. Bad deeds only count once, so we can easily outdo them in these modern times for which the Message of Islam is meant. The service prayer is obligatory (Fardh) for anyone above the age of 10. During the prayer one isn't allowed to interrupt or speak to anyone.

Of course, it is permitted to do many more prayers, if wanted. One can also address Allah at any time even without washing, respectfully, praise Him, thank Him, and ask Him for forgiveness, consolation, hope, guidance, and progress in all matters of life, as and when required. It is important to keep Allah in remembrance in all matters of life and mention His name before beginning to eat, sleep, etc. There are Duas, prayers, for that and His 99 names.

The prayer times are synchronised with the natural clock and described in the Quran. From the first light to sunrise (Fajr), shortly after the zenith (Dhohor), during the afternoon when the sun is at an angle of 45 degrees (Asr), shortly after sunset (Maghrib) and at night (Isha). Shortly after sunrise and shortly before sunset prostration isn't permitted as in ancient times some people used to worship the sun in this way.

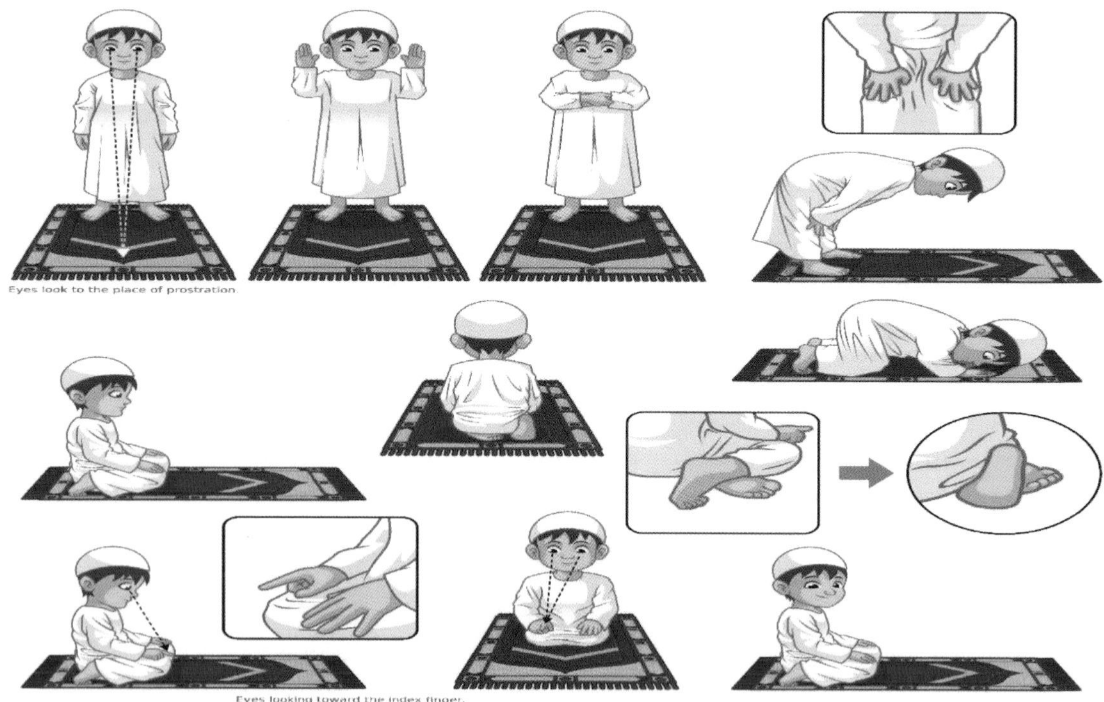

Salah (Service Prayer)

In the morning (Fajr) there are 2 periods (Rakahs), midday (Dhohor) has 4, afternoon (Asr) there are also 4, evening (Maghrib) there are 3, and at night (Isha) there are 4. These are the obligatory (Fardh) prayers. One can do more voluntary prayers.

Adhan (Times and Call)

During travels one should combine the midday and afternoon prayers and conduct them in the afternoon by doing 2 periods for each of them, see below. One should also put together the evening and night-prayers in the evening and shorten the night-prayer by 2 periods. In other words, Fajr stays as it is, Dhohor and Asr are done at Asr-time and shortened to 2 Rakahs each and Maghrib and Isha are done at Maghrib time and Isha is shortened to 2 Rakahs as well. Voluntary prayers are before or afterwards (Sunnah and Nafil). More times for voluntary prayers are before sleep (Witr, uneven number of Rakahs), after midnight or early in the morning (Tahajjud, even number of Rakahs) and 15 minutes after sunrise (Subha). During their monthly periods and up to 40 days after giving birth, women are not supposed to conduct the ritual-prayer due to the weakness caused by the loss of blood.

The call to prayer (Adhan) is done by the Moazzin using the human voice rather than bells or horns and one is supposed to echo it: „Allahu Akbar" (Allah is the Greatest), 4x, “Ashhadu an la ilaha ill-llah" (I witness there is no deity apart from Allah) 2x, „Ashhadu anna Mohammadur Rasoul ul-llah" (I witness that Mohammed is the Messenger of Allah) 2x, „Hai’a alas Salah" (Come to Prayer) 2x, „Hai’a alal Falah" (Come to success) 2x, Allahu Akbar" (Allah is the Greatest) 2x, “La ilaha ill-llah” (No deity apart from Allah) 1x. For Fajr-Adhan one adds “As Salatu khairum menan Naom” (Prayer is better than sleep) 2x, after “Hai’a alal Falah". Shortly before each prayer comes another call (the Iqaamah) where one repeats the Adhan and adds “Qad qaamatis Salah” (The prayer is beginning) 2x after “Hai’a alal Falah”. The first call to prayer was given by Bilal, a companion of Prophet, pbuh, who came from Abyssinia/Africa.

Salah (Service Prayer)

The service-prayer is a duty that has certain etiquettes and mannerism. There are different positions and invocations that follow a certain principle of praise, gratitude, and forgiveness. These are conducted ritualistically and regularly in a certain chronology as obligated and ordained to our Prophet Mohammed, PBUH.

Positions

The obligatory (Fardh) prayers should ideally be done in congregation and in the mosque standing in rows, shoulder to shoulder, foot to foot. The different positions as mentioned before Quran and emphasized in the Hadith. One are also mentioned in the precondition for the completion of the prayer is a healthy state of mind and body. Ideally one should be sober and clean washed. People with injuries or disabilities are allowed to sit on a chair or stay in a kneeling position. In case of fear or paralyses one can pray even just moving the eyes or only in thought. In the mosque, the Imam leads the prayer and one follows his voice.

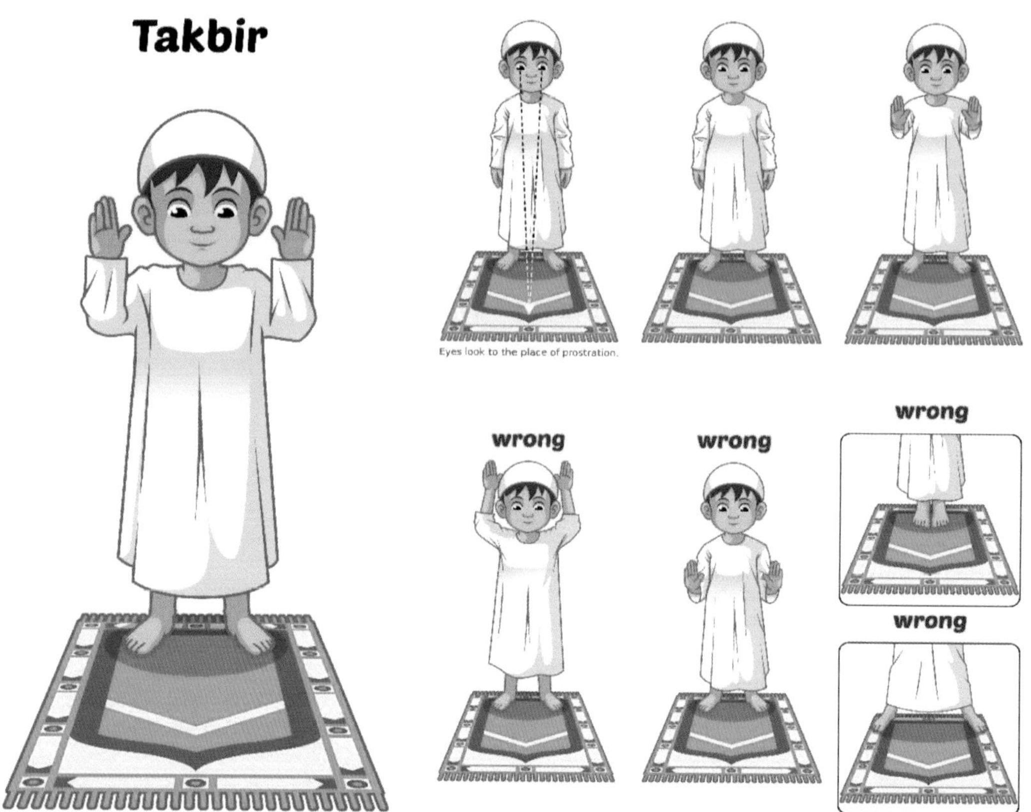

Qiyam (Standing)

After the Iqaamah and with the Takbeer, Allahu Akbar" (Allah is the Greatest) the worshipper lifts the arms and hands above the ears. This stretches the triceps. Then one moves them back, which stretches the biceps and breast/ shoulders, afterwards one binds the hands together between breast and navel. The worshipper can press down on the diaphragm and pull them apart, grabbing right hand above the left, which tones the upper back and shoulders as well. One should take posture, meaning tummy in, shoulders down, upper body erect and head looking slightly down towards the floor around one body length in front of the feet. The feet should be shoulder-wider apart and straight. During this standing position the introduction is whispered first: “Subhanaka Allah-umma wa behamdeka, wa tabarakasmoka, wata’ala jaddoka, wa laila’ha ghairoka, a’udhobillahi menash-shaitannir-rajeem, Bismillah-ir Rahmaan-ir Raheem.”

Salah (Service Prayer)

During the Iqaamah the worshippers line up in rows standing shoulder to shoulder, feet to feet and with the Takbeer the prayer begins by lifting the hands above the ears and tying them together, right hand above the left. The Imam leads the prayer.

Qiyam (Standing)

All Glory "The introduction mentioned on the previous page means: is to You Allah, and all praised for You, blessed be Your Name and exalted Your Majesty and there is no deity apart from you. I seek refuge with Allah from Satan the cursed. In Glory Allah's Most Forgiving, Full of Mercy." In this way the worshippers address Allah and then recite the Opening Surah of the Quran (Surah Al-Fatiha), after which follows a part of a long Surah in the first Rakah and short Surahs in the following Rakahs. After that follows the Takbeer (Allah-u Akbar, Allah is the Greatest, always while changing positions) and then the...

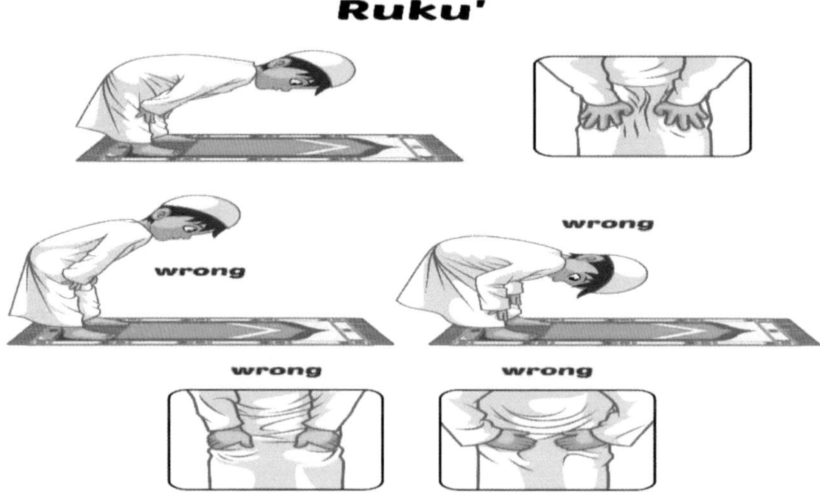

Rukuh (Bowing)

After lifting the hands over the ears, the worshipper bows down and places the hands on the knee-caps and continuous to gaze on the same spot as before in front of him/her. This position has extremely beneficial effect on the blood circulation and the back, which is stretched. It is said that the word Rukuh also stands for a certain artery that opens in this position and increases the blood flow to a particular part of the brain that is responsible for spirituality and faith. One praises Allah saying, “Subhana Rabbial Azeem”, meaning, “Praised be the Exalted Guardian". There are more invocations for this position and scholars say that this position is for gratitude, so one should try to collect the thoughts about the blessings Allah has given. This is merely symbolical, as one cannot be grateful enough for all the favours Allah has done. In general, all invocations are whispered, because the angels cannot read our thoughts and Allah wants them as a witness. That is a mystery of creation and will be dealt with in a separate book. Satan tries to distract you from your prayer by reminding you of embarrassing memories or movies you might have watched. Anytime during the prayer, the way to avoid that is by blowing three times over your left shoulder and saying “La hauwla wa la quwata illah Billah”, which means “there is now power nor deity other than through Allah”.

You must keep trying this for some time until Satan gives up.

Sujud

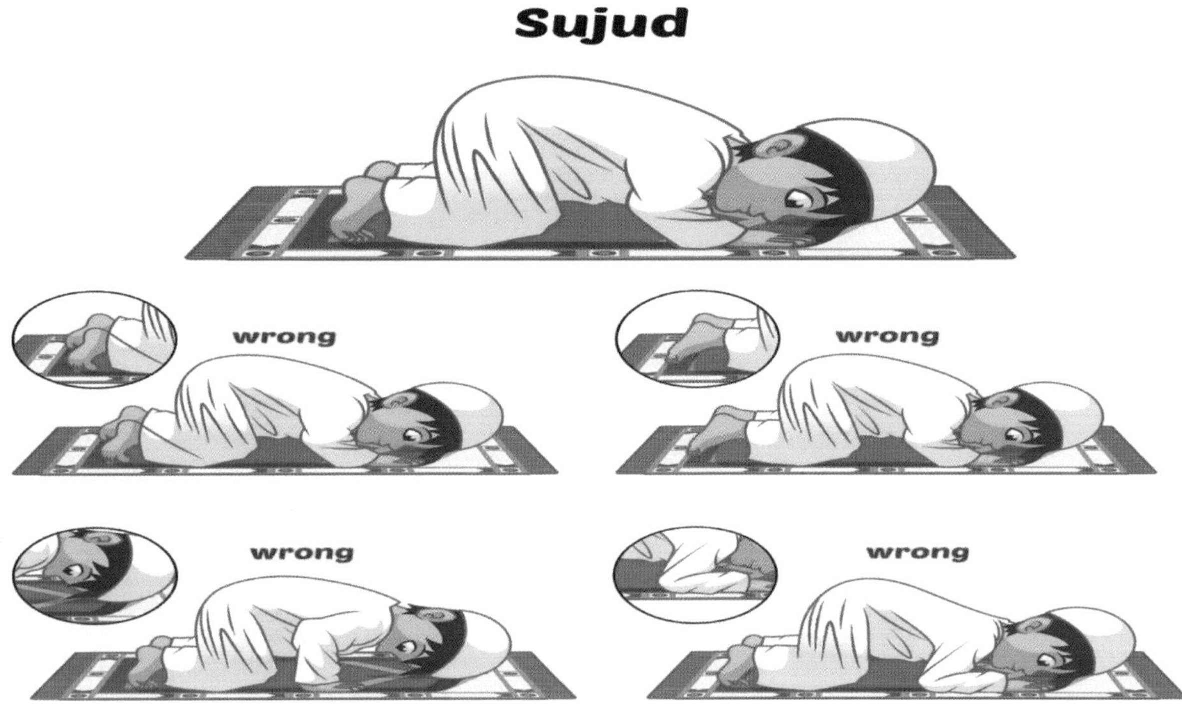

Salah (Service Prayer)

The Earth is the place of our biological origin and Allah has created us from it and placed us on it. When we touch it, Satan sees us as insignificant and not as a challenge; because he believes he is superior as he is created from fire/energy.

Sajdah (Transition to Prostration)

-Same Allah"The bowing position or Rukuh is ended with the saying: oleman hameda", which means, “Allah hears the one who praises Him", and one changes briefly into the standing position, Rafi'a min ar-ruku, with hands either tied or held downward along the sides of Rabbana wa lakal hamd, hamdan kasiran "the body and recites: mujeebaan mobaarakan fihi mil as-samawaate wa mil al ardhe wa mil a ma baina homa wa mil a ma she’ta min shaeim baad", Guardian, praised be you with praises plentiful and "meaning, blessed, to fill the heavens and the earth and all in between and fill Rabbana wa "all that will please You besides these" or short just Guardian, praise be to You"."lakal hamd",

With a Takbeer the Imam now gets down on his knees or knees and hands and then prostrates by placing his flat palms with fingers other next to his ears on the floor and his closed touching each forehead and nose on the floor where he was looking at before. The congregation of worshippers follows him. In this position the elbows should not touch the floor and the tiptoes are bent to lay flat on the ground while the feet are upright stretching away from it in a right angle to train the tendons. One can push against the floor with the hands to train the arm muscles or the head against the floor to train the neck.

There are many fine nuances and details of all the positions, and they are also very subjective. There are different schools of thought that pray slightly differently. Everyone develops his/her own style over time within limits and one can trains to be very thorough and focussed.

Salah (Service Prayer)

The prostration symbolises the return to the origin, the floor, the earth, the state of unity with nature, Allah's creation. Our Prophet Mohammed, pbuh, said that during the prostration a servant moves closest to Allah. If we feel very tempted by Satan to do evil or he is mocking us or making us feel sad, we can always go into the Sajdah and plead to Allah for protection after saying: “Aoudhobillahe Menash-Shaitan-irrajeem” (I seek refuge with Allah from Satan the cursed).

Sajdah (Prostration)

(Praise be "During the prostration one says "Subhana-Rabbial-Ala to the Guardian Supreme) three times. Now it is time to seek for forgiveness for the mistakes (sins) one has made. Allah forgives even the small sins a person doesn't remember, as long as he or she shows remorse. Regarding big sins like murder, adultery and exploitation one should really do everything to avoid them. If they still happen, it is a matter between Allah and His servant if they can be forgiven. In any case, one has to do many good deeds! (That is why good deeds count 10-fold, and during Ramdhan they even count 100 or 1000-fold!). But in principle, Allah wants to forgive every sin, apart from one: Shirk. Allah is forgiving and merciful in all cases apart from this one. Apart from forgiveness, one can also ask for guidance, progress, and success with regards to worldly (duniya) and spiritual (aakhirah) matters. After the prostration one follows the kneeling position and another prostration. Every change in position is begun with a Takbeer (Allah-u Akbar, Allah is the Greatest). One period (Rakah) consists of the standing position, the bowing, the first prostration and the second prostration. Afterwards, one stands back up and the next period (Rakah) follows. If one can stand up from the kneeling position without using the arms, it strengthens the legs.

Salah (Service Prayer)

One can also place the hands on the floor before standing up and rise from the prostration in that way, especially after the first Rakah, because the joints aren't warmed up yet. 8 points touch the floor: Both tiptoes of the feet, both knees, both hands with fingers pulled together (keep the elbows lifted) and the nose and the forehead.

Sajdah (Prostration)

Many worshippers forget the second kneeling during the first and third Rakah, which is very short and has a special prayer:

"Allahuma aghfirli Warhamni Wahdini Wajuburni Waafini Warzuqni Warafaani" (O Allah! Forgive me, have mercy on me, guide me, support me, protect me, give me sustenance, raise me up.) Very often the prayer is shortened and rushed. It is better to take your time because Allah appreciates that. Every prayer should be as focussed as if it was the last. While in prostration, the toes should be stretched so that the blood supply to the feet and calves increases. If one decreases the distance between head and knees one can train the core muscles, the flexibility of the backbone, and shrink the stomach. If you push the hands hard against the floor, you can train biceps and triceps. Also, the lung volume increases if you take deep breaths. Blood rushes to the head and the sense of balance is trained. By breathing small amounts of dust through your nose which touches the floor, you fortify your body against allergies and your immune system against infections. The forehead which also touches the floor contains the part of the brain where sinful thoughts occur, (Surah 96, Verse 16), e.g lies and so on. You could picture the sins being drawn into the earth while Allah forgives them. Try to think of Allah and make tawbah (repentance)!

Salah (Service Prayer)

While kneeling the stretch of the thighs contributes to strengthening the immune system. The worshipper kneels between the two prostrations and before standing up, which means that he or she stands up from the kneeling position!

Knees and Fitness

After two rakahs one remains in the kneeling position for longer and speaks certain prayers and the Shahadah (Testimony):

"Ashhadu al-Lailaha-illa-llahu, Wa Ashhadu anna Mohammadan Abdohu Warosulohu" (I testify there is no other deity than Allah and I testify that Mohammed is His servant and Messenger.) Therewhile the hands are placed on the knees and one can press them down, pull the arms and shoulders back to improve the upper back posture. Most people forget that, but it needs to be trained. During the shahadah the right pointer-finger is lifted symbolising the oneness of Allah. This position is for praying for the Ummah (people of the Prophet Momammed, pbuh, and also Abraham's folks, pbuh (Durud Sharif). Then one prays for protection from hellfire and the trials of this world. (Rabbana Aatena fi Dunya hassantun wal Achirate hassantun waqaina azab An Naar).

After the morning prayer which consists of two rakahs the greeting follows over the right and left shoulder (Assalaamo Alaikum wa rahmat Ullah) to the fellow worshippers and the angels sitting on the shoulders witnessing good and bad deeds, the one on the right, writes down the good deeds, and the one on the left, writes the bad deeds. During prayers that last longer than two Rakahs the worshipper stands up after the shahadah and continues with the prayer for the Ummah at the end of the fourth Rakah. Now the prayer is finished, and one concludes with Dhikr (remembrance) of Allah and Dua'as (pleading prayers). It is important for your health to exercise regularly, and the prayer becomes easier then, as well as reading the Quran. Our Prophet Mohammed (pbuh) walked to the mosque five times a day and exercised when riding and practicing other sports.

The different positions of the service-prayer help with the digestion of food. The way the food passes through the stomach and guts is aided by the sequence of the movements, especially the bowing and prostration.

Zakat (Alms)

These consist of 5-10% of the harvest or 2.5% of the annual savings and are meant for the poor, desolate, homeless, hungry, travellers, beggars and for poor family members.

Amount and Ribah (Usury)

In the Hadith, our Prophet, pbuh, said that in case of agricultural produce there is 5-10% due, for example in case of land that needs to be irrigated 5% has to be given away and in case of land, that has adjacent rivers or canals for irrigation it is 10%. If you are employed, some scholars say it is only 2.5% of your savings left over every year after expenditure. Apart from these compulsory alms, there is also Businesspeople who have highly (Sadqah). voluntary charity profitable dealings should invest more back into the community for charitable purposes. This also guarantees a healthy society and environment for their business as well as ensuring their raw material supply, employee welfare and blessings from Allah. Obviously, it is our duty as representatives of Allah on earth to ensure a healthy environment and economical as well as ecological dealings (Surah 2, Verse 30 and Surah 55, Verse 9). One should give away openly and secretly as Allah says in the Quran. It should be openly to motivate others and not to boast with it and secretly to ensure the blessings from Allah. One should ask for forgiveness in case one might feel that one is better than the one receiving the charity. Usury (high interest at exploitative rates, see Surah 2, Verse 275-278) is forbidden in Islam.

In combination with the alms this ensures a just society and prevents inflation and crisis. Clearly alms are an effective way of alleviating poverty and aim for equality. In fact, it is said in the Hadith that charity doesn't diminish one's salary. You will receive it back in ways of blessings. It can also consist of emotional support and other types of help and doesn't have to be money, necessarily, like social service and helping with cleaning and lifting goods. Kind words, counselling someone, cancelling and paying off debt of others are also a form of charity.

Sawm (Fasting)

The month of Ramadhan is for fasting, which means that you don't eat or drink during the daylight hours. Fasting serves to strengthen your faith and body, improves your health and teach you self-control to move closer to Allah. Viruses and bacteria don’t like a fasting body, so you are also protected better against diseases.

Ramadhan

In the Islamic Calendar the month of Ramadhan is the month, during which the Quran was revealed to our Prophet Mohammed, pbuh. That was a miracle from Allah as the Prophet, pbuh, could not read or write at that time, which would have made it impossible for him to write and learn such long texts by heart, being an illiterate. The words were revealed to him via the Archangel Gabriel and written into his heart. Mohammed, pbuh, related the messages to his fellow humans and practiced the laws ordained perfectly to be a good example for us all.

One of the orders in the Quran relates to fasting from sunrise to sunset as a symbol of gratitude for the Quran, and it is compulsory for the Muslims. During this time, one isn't allowed to eat or drink from sunrise to sunset and should also pay special attention to behaviour and self-control, even more than usual. The rules of fasting are complex, but the advantages are clear: One learns to take control over one's physical desires; one strengthens their faith, because fasting with a weak faith is difficult. Therefore, the nearness to Allah becomes tangible. It is said that Satan is in chains and hell freezes over, and Allah moves close the first heaven to rejoice about the worship of His servants. The worshipper develops empathy for the poor and hungry and is encouraged to give charity. Good deeds count 100-fold during Ramadhan and even 1000 fold during the last 10 days. There is a special night called Laylatul-Qadr (the Night of Destiny, Surah 97), when a prayer counts like 1000 months of prayer. During Ramdhan there are special collective prayers in the mosque called Taraawih (Restfulness) when the Quran is completed during the 30 nights in congregation and the text is reaffirmed as well as the bond with Allah and in between the believers. There is a special vibe and the presence of the angels, and the good spirits can be felt, if you develop sensitivity for these by submitting to Allah and dedicating your life to Him. He will bless you with success in this life and the hereafter, in sha Allah (if Allah wills).

Sawm (Fasting)

Fasting strengthens your body and spirit and prevents illness. It also increases your life expectancy and the quality of life. Allah loves the fasting worshipper and hears the prayers of the servant.

Advantages

It is medically proven that fasting does the body much good, the rest for the stomach, the return of the appetite, the stand still of digestion, etc. The lack of calories diminishes the bad cholesterol and frees the blood vessels from toxins and blockage.

If you drink without eating, you create a lack of electrolytes and risk cramps and a headache. Also, by not drinking you increase the dehydration tolerance. Many people say that not drinking water all day is unhealthy, but this is just temporarily and sometime beneficial. Continuing your fast into the night is disadvantageous because the hypophysis creates hormones that make it easier to fast during daylight. Before the time of Our Prophet Mohammed, pbuh, people fasted into the night, and he also did it, but asked us not to do it.

Fasting is ideal for the human body and increases life expectancy. The performance can enhance during the fast because you are not spending any energy on digestion and won't feel bloated and under the burden of digestion. Some Muslim sportsmen play their best matches during Ramadhan while fasting. Our Prophet Mohammed, pbuh, also fasted outside Ramadhan on Mondays and Thursdays.

The daylight hours vary greatly across the world and between the arctic circles and the poles daylight vanishes for 6 months and lasts for 6 months during the arctic winters and summers, so no fasting is possible unless you take the time of the nearest cities beyond the arctic circles. Ramadhan moves over the solar year as it goes with the lunar year. It moves back approximately 10 days each year and moves across all seasons. So, in cold countries it can be during summer and winter, and it can be from 20 hours long in summer to less than 7 hours short in winter!

One should pray for forgiveness and focussing becomes easier during Ramadhan with a little practice, just like all intellectual and mental engagement. Allah also fulfils the prayers if they are useful and beneficial for us. Allah loves the fasting worshipper, and he will be forgiven, in any case. The last 10 days are especially blessed and fasting can become a little more difficult. One should not overeat and eat healthy after breaking the fast in the evening after sunset and hydrate well.

Sawm (Fasting)

While fasting, the blood values improve tremendously. Ramadhan happens at different times of the year and at the end there is the Eid festival, when a lot of alms are given, and feasts take place.

Times

Our Prophet Mohammed, pbuh, has told his companions when repeatedly asked about the best fasting that David's, pbuh, fast was the best, who fasted every second day. It is proven now that the blood values of those who fast every second day are the best, even better than fasting every day consecutively. This is another scientific sign. But the fast during Ramdhan is the right one for modern days and our Prophet, pbuh, didn't recommend fasting like David, pbuh. The worshipper rises before sunrise and eats and drinks. It can be as early as 2.30 am in Europe during summers and as late as 7.30 am in winter. The fast is broken after sunset, which can be as late as 10.30 pm in summer in Europe and as early as 4.30 pm in winter. As Ramadhan moves back about 10 days each year, it returns to the same season every 36-37 years. The closer you get to the equator, the less the difference between summer and winter. An average human experiences Ramdhan in each season. In any case, breaking the fast is an exhilarating experience and the taste buds enjoy every moment of it. At the end of Ramdhan, the first Eid (Eid-al-Fitr) is celebrated. It is combined with social gatherings, feasts, colourful new clothes and alms giving to the poor in general and also pocket money for the younger family members. It is a colourful experience on the streets of Muslim countries. Ramdhan lasts from one new moon to the next and the sighting of the new moon sickle introduces Ramdhan and Eid. It is the Sunnah of our Prophet Mohammed, pbuh, to fast on after Eid for 6-7 days. Fasting on Eid day is forbidden though. It is said that the reward for fasting before and after Ramdhan is like fasting the whole year! The second Eid (Eid-al-Adha) festival is at the end of the Haj-pilgrimage on the day of sacrifice (see below).

Haj (Pilgrimage)

During the Haj, the pilgrim walks in the footsteps of Abraham, pbuh, and his wife Hajra, pbuh, who settled in Mecca with their son Ishmael, pbuh. She found water there.

Mecca, Tawaaf and Umrah

During the month of Dhul-Haj the annual pilgrimage takes place, which every Muslim should perform once in his life, if he or she can afford it. The Umrah, which is part of the Haj, consists of a few of the rituals and can be done all year long. The pilgrim visits Mecca and the Kaaba, which is the first house of God and the common direction of prayer built by Abraham and his son Ishmael, pbut, and performs a Tawaaf, which means he or she circumambulates them anti-clockwise seven times and performs 2 Nafil Rakah prayers. This with 3 times running between Safa and Marwa (the hills that Hajrah, pbuh, wandered between in search of water. The beginning and end point of the Tawaaf is the footstep of Abraham, pbuh, which is imprinted into cement. One also tried to kiss or throw a kiss towards the hajr-ul-aswad (as per Sunnah), the black stone which is a meteorite that Allah sent as a miracle from the seventh heaven to assist Abraham, pbuh like an elevator while building the Kaaba.

The anti-clockwise, mathematical positive circumambulation represents the laws and origins of the universe, such as the electrons, the moons, the planets and the galaxies, which all spin in the same direction. The angels also circumambulate Allah in this manner. Before commencing the pilgrimage-zone in Mecca (the Miqaat), the pilgrim puts on the Ihram (simple, white cloth without stitching worn like a tunic), which is wound around the hips and thrown over the left shoulder. Women wear a garment which covers the head. Men aren't allowed to cover the head or to shave until finished. The pilgrim is in the state of celibacy (no intercourse). Rich and poor and all races are the same in the crowd. The Umrah consists of the Tawaaf and visiting the Zamzam, the source of water discovered by Hajrah and Ishmael, pbut.

According to the Hadith, baby Ishmael, pbuh, was scratching the earth which Hajrah, pbuh, was running between the hills Safa and Marwah in search of water. Ishmael, pbuh, managed to scratch open the source. By running between the hills, men now pay thanks for this motherly care symbolically. One drinks from the Zamzam water, which has healing and purifying properties.

Haj (Pilgrimage)

The pilgrim fulfils certain rituals and is dressed in Ihram for three days, which means he or she also refuses to intercourse, argument, perfumes, and scented creams. The Haj purifies the soul and you become innocent like a child.

Rituals, Sacrifice and Locations

During the Haj, the pilgrim first enters Mina (a city outside Mecca, see below). Then he or she travels to the plain of Arafat, where mankind will be collected on the last day and where our Prophet Mohammed, pbuh, held his last sermon. The day is spent praying and then there is a journey to Muzdalfah, where the elephant army of the Abyssinian King Abra was stopped from marching to Mecca by a flock of finches who bombarded them with clay stones (Surah Al Fil, 105). That happened shortly before Mohammed's, pbuh, birth and the Kaaba was under threat. He prayed there all night for the forgiveness of all Muslims. The Umrah follows and then the pilgrim returns to Mina where Abraham, pbuh, was supposed to sacrifice his first-born son, Ismael, pbuh, according to a dream. Satan tried to prevent him from going to the place of sacrifice. Abraham, pbuh, stoned him and Satan because stone. The stone columns called Jamarat that are standing in that very place are stoned by the pilgrim with 3 x 7 stones. Now the sacrifice of an animal follows because Ishmael, pbuh, was replaced by a lamb. After the stoning, a sacrifice follows. Then men shave their heads and women cut off one curl from their hair. If you cannot afford to make a sacrifice, you can fast that day. (Originally one was supposed to raise the animal and show love for it, so that the sacrifice puts the love for Allah above the love for the animal. Sacrifice and eating meat was originally limited to Eid and birth of children. This has ecological and physiological benefits, as well minimising the suffering of animals.)

Now the Ihram is taken off. Women travel to do the Haj with their husbands, brothers, fathers or sons, a Mehram. They can also travel in a group. Mecca is at the centre point of the golden ratio of all land (this is also a miracle). In this way, Islam could spread evenly across all land in all directions. All Muslims can still travel relatively easily to get there to this day, as it is central to all of them.

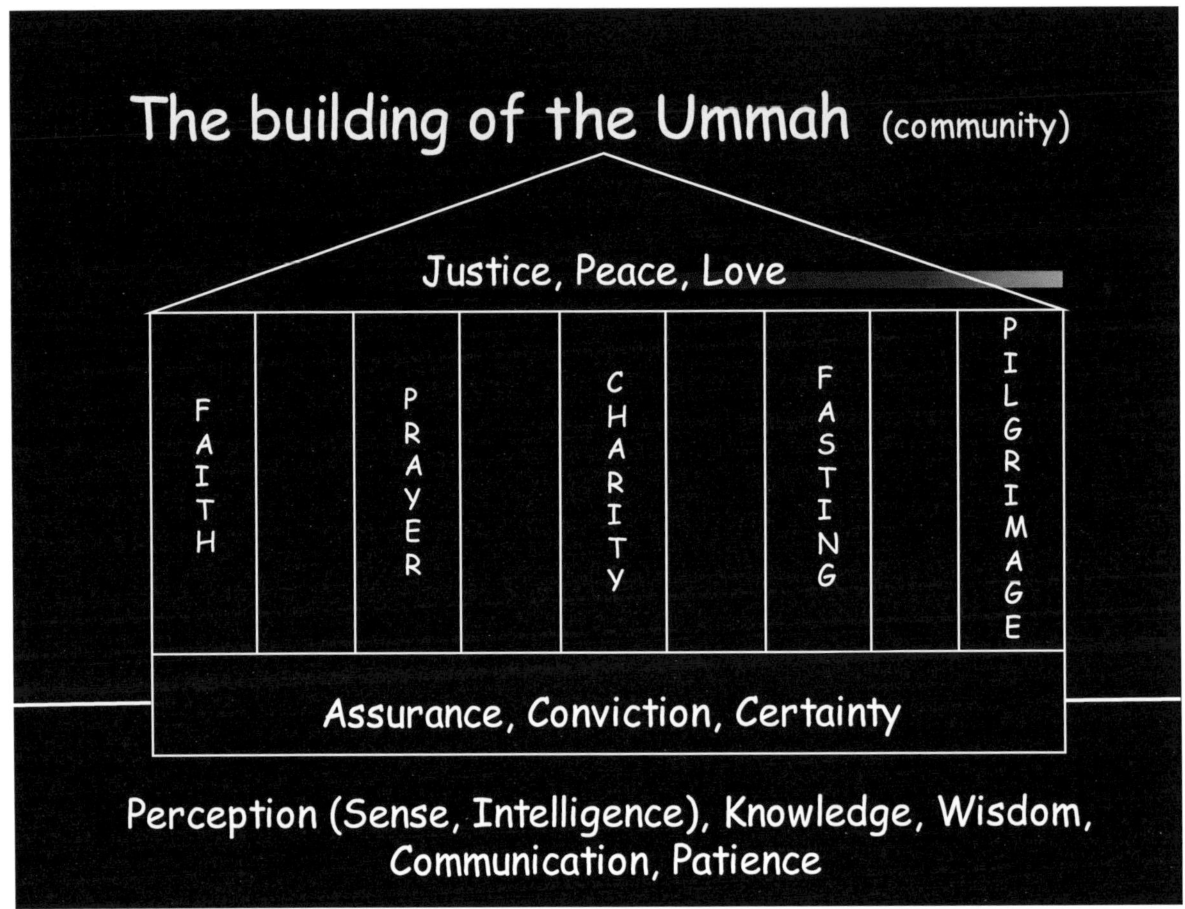

Justice (Economical and Ecological)

One of the intentions of the 5 pillars, apart from worshipping Allah, is to achieve social justice in relation to the economy and the environment.

Iman = Conviction, Certainty and Assurance

Salah (Service-Prayer) = Gratitude, Forgiveness, Guidance and Progress/Success

Zakat (Alms) = Charity, Love and Equality

Sawm (Fasting) = Self-control, Discipline and Tolerance

Haj (Pilgrimage) = Purification, Hardship, Sacrifice

Sense, Sensibility and Reason are the Sunnah (habit) of Allah. The last resort is violence or punishment, forgiveness and mercy are much better. War and fighting are to be avoided at all costs, diplomacy and compromise are better unless one is attacked or suppressed relentlessly. Overconsumption, overproduction, and waste are a big sin. Only acting in this manner can we expect Allah's reward and ultimate happiness when we treat those under and around us with care. We are Allah's representants on the earth and we are asked to sustain His creation (Surah 55). We have been given the power to destroy it or preserve it. As Muslims we are supposed to preserve it.

"I testify that there is no deity other than Allah And I testify that Mohammed is Allah's Servant and Messenger!"

Printed in Great Britain
by Amazon